THE HIDDEN LIFE
OF THE SOUL

From the French

BY THE AUTHOR OF " A DOMINICAN ARTIST," " LIFE
OF MADAME LOUISE DE FRANCE," ETC. ETC.

" Our life is hid with Christ in God"

RIVINGTONS
London, Oxford, and Cambridge
1870

Preface

THE author from whose writings the following chapters on the interior life are taken, was himself deeply and practically versed in the subject on which he wrote. While leading many souls along its blessed ways, his own life, so far as the world is concerned, was altogether "hid with Christ in God." Profoundly learned, not only as a theologian, but also as a classical student, the earnest devoutness of his mind (which was at once deep and broad) taught him to humble the power of a large and cultivated intellect before the Faith of Christ with the simplicity of a little child. Jean Nicolas Grou's writings are characterised by an absence of exaggeration which gives peculiar weight to his teaching. Love of God is the mainspring by which he would rule the whole Christian life; his motto

is ever "the Love of Christ constraineth us."
Through the tender yet firm constraint of that
love, he seeks to draw the soul to a perfectly simple
surrender of self, which is to lead on to that life of
which St. Paul said, "I live, yet not I, but Christ
liveth in me." It is a life in which the soul " asks
nothing and refuses nothing," desiring only in all
things to fulfil God's holy Will. That the author's
language should have led to the charge of Quietism
is scarcely to be wondered at, in spite of his own as-
surance that he had no sympathy whatever with
that enervating form of religious error. But those
who will take the Père Grou as a spiritual guide,
and study his teaching thoughtfully and prayerfully,
will find themselves upon a track of earnest stedfast devotion, sober and unexciting rather than
sensational or extraordinary, but certainly not
"passive," in the sense of neglecting the call to
"work out our own salvation," while subjecting
every effort to God's holy Will and pleasure.

In these days, when excitement is perhaps the
prevailing danger, not only of our material but of

our spiritual life, it has been thought that some souls may find rest and strength in the simple words of advice with which Père Grou supplied those who looked to him for guidance in the restless period which preceded the great Revolution.

It would be incorrect to say of a man who lived in such times that his years were uneventful; and yet Jean Nicolas Grou's life leaves us with an impression of calmness and tranquillity, in spite of its manifold troubles, ending as they did with exile and a lingering death in a foreign land. But thoughout that life the questions, "What profit?" and "What matter?" were answered practically by "I count all things but loss for the excellency of the knowledge of Christ Jesus my Lord."

There is not much to tell of the outward incidents of Père Grou's life. He was born at Calais in 1731, and educated by the Jesuit Fathers. Study and devotion (under which head we must include the guidance of souls) filled up his life, whether in Paris, or in Lorraine—where the Duke Stanislas sheltered him during a period of trial which preceded the outbreak of the great Revolution—or in Holland, or in England, whither, in the year 1792, he finally retired before the rapidly advancing waves of that terrible tempest. The Père Grou was the author of various works, classical as well as theological. One of the latter, " Traité dogmatique de la vraie religion," undertaken at the request of Monseigneur de Beaumont, Archbishop of Paris, and costing fourteen years of labour, was burnt at Paris some time later. On receiving the tidings, Père Grou's only remark was, "If the work could serve God, He would preserve it; but He will make use of some other more profitable servant than I am, to promote His glory."

In the year 1792, the Rev. Mr. Clinton, chaplain to Mr. Weld of Lulworth, invited him to seek a refuge in England ; and for a time the exile shared Father Clinton's quarters, whence after a while he moved to the Castle, at Mr. Weld's earnest desire. A devoted friendship between the Weld family and Père Grou seems to have lasted during the

remaining years of his life; but notwithstanding
the good Father's affection for his hosts and their
children, he continued to live in an almost perpetual retreat. Prayer and writing occupied all
the time which was not claimed by his minis-
terial duties. He never began to write without
praying that his work might be blessed, nor can
we wonder that he believed himself to be guided
by God to labour for His glory. " I write nothing
of myself," he says; "God directs my pen; I
often take it up not knowing what I am about
to say, and sometimes I marvel at the thoughts
suggested to me. If God gives me '*de quoi*,' I write
freely; if not, I wait His will." During his latter
years he ceased to write, saying that " God did not
give him *de quoi*."

This calm studious life lasted for ten years,
during which the Père Grou was only once induced
to leave Lulworth, and join a circle of congenial
minds at Wardour Castle. But even this he felt
to be a distraction, and the experiment was never
repeated. In 1802 his health gave way to such

an extent that on Christmas Eve, after cele-
brating his first two masses, he could not proceed
with the third. From that time he was unable to
stand or lie, but remained for the rest of his life
sitting in an arm-chair, where however he continued to hear confessions, and to edify all who
had the privilege of seeing him by his patience
and serenity, and his continual fervent preparation
for death. The Rev. Mr. Brooke (then Mr. Weld's
chaplain) used to bring him the Blessed Sacrament, and spend much time with him; but he
was accustomed to say that Père Grou lived too
wholly with God to need any human companion-
ship.

On the 13th December 1803, his end being
visibly near, Père Grou received the last Sacraments, and shortly after departed this life peace-
fully and painlessly, exclaiming almost with his
last breath, " My God, it is indeed sweet to die
in Thine Arms."

Père Grou once said in confidence to one of his
spiritual children, that the greatest grace God had

ever given him was a childlike and simple spirit, the
lack of which, as he thought, had previously closed
his eyes to the deep things of God. "Now," he
added, with his characteristic humility, "I see a
little more plainly, and I am able to perceive how
impossible it would have been for me to bear the
trials with which it has pleased God to visit me,
had He not mercifully made me to be but as a
little child before Him."

Such a childlike spirit, and how to attain it, as
gathered from instructions given to those who con-
sulted him, is the main teaching of this volume.
This spirit underlies his whole thought. "All
peace and happiness in this world depend upon
unreserved self-oblation to God;"—and this willing and perfect offering is to be made, not through
great or extraordinary efforts, but in "little things,
which come daily, hourly, within our reach." He
loved to inculcate simplicity; freedom from all
affectation and unreality; the patience and humility
which are too surely grounded in self-knowledge to
be surprised at a fall, but withal so allied to confi-

dence in God, as to make recovery easy and sure.
While Père Grou insisted that our wills should be
bent in unfeigned submission to the Will of God,
he nevertheless put forward confidence, generosity,
and a childlike spirit as the groundwork of the
spiritual life rather than external mortifications
or ascetic devotion. "The outer life of a really
devout man should be thoroughly attractive to
others," according to this teaching; and that, because it ought to be "simple, honest, straightforward, unpretending, gentle, kindly, cheerful and
sensible, . . . indulgent to all save sin" (p. 12).
Yet this simple, and at first sight ordinary rule of
conduct is not to be treated as an easy matter,
lightly achieved. "Many a year of struggle" has to
be spent in seeking the detachment which it involves,
and the soul must be led onwards by Divine Light to
face the weighty questions, "What God asks of us?"
and "What we should ask of God?" before dying to
self it can rise to "the new Life in Jesus Christ."
And then, "Let Him do with His children as He
will, let Him prove them or comfort them, let Him

seem to hide His Face, or visibly have them in His holy keeping, their souls will alike be at rest." Externally they may be tossed hither and thither;—"all Thy waves and storms are gone over me; but there is peace within" (p. 70). "God only," is the result of every rule, every effort. And we may well believe that as the venerable priest passed to his rest with those touching words upon his lips, " My God, it is indeed sweet to die in Thine Arms," his heart re-echoed the summary he has left us of all his teaching, " No more self, no more of this world,

" GOD ONLY."

" BLESSED IS THE MAN WHOSE STRENGTH IS IN THEE: IN WHOSE HEART ARE THY WAYS; WHO GOING THROUGH THE VALE OF MISERY USE IT FOR A WELL, AND THE POOLS ARE FILLED WITH WATER. THEY WILL GO FROM STRENGTH TO STRENGTH . . . .

"O LORD GOD OF HOSTS, BLESSED IS THE MAN THAT PUTTETH HIS TRUST IN THEE."

Contents

The Foundations of the Hidden Life

GOD has given us the "law of perfect liberty," to the end that we should use it to His service; and that liberty is never so safe as when we trust it unreservedly to Him, setting self-will aside, and leaving all to Him : " for we know that all things work together for good to them that love God." Self-rule will probably err. Moreover, those who choose their own path must be responsible for the consequences thereof, however serious ; whereas when God rules, we need nothing save patient trust. He loves us far more than we can love ourselves, and He watches over us with more than a Father's love. Trust in Him, and it is impossible for devil or man to hinder His grace.

All peace and happiness in this world depend upon unreserved self-oblation to God. If this be hearty and entire, the result will be an unfailing, ever-increasing happiness, which nothing can disturb. There is no real happiness in this life, save

that which is the result of a peaceful heart; and
Holy Scripture tells us that "there is no peace to
the wicked." Even religious people who only half
give themselves up to God, know but feebly what
this peace is;—they are easily disturbed by many
things, scruples, dread of God's judgments, or the
changes and chances of life. But the soul which
gives itself wholly and without reserve to God, is
filled with His Own Peace; and inasmuch as we
are prone to grow like that to which we are closely
united, the closer we draw to our God so much the
stronger and more stedfast and more tranquil shall
we become. Those who cleave to the things of this
world are for ever tossed about with the waves and
storms of uncertainty—God Alone is Immoveable,
Unchangeable, and he who trusts in Him will never
be confounded.

Of our own strength we are equally incapable of
great works or small, but it is safest to aim at the
lesser, leaving God to call us to serve Him in greater
things, when He may see fit. Meanwhile, little
things come daily, hourly, within our reach, and
they are not less calculated to set forward our
growth in holiness, than are the greater occasions
which occur but rarely;—in some ways we may
turn them to more profit, inasmuch as they do not

war against humility, or tend to feed self-conceit.
Moreover, fidelity in trifles, and an earnest seeking
to please God in little matters, is a test of real devotion and love. It is quite possible to perform very
ordinary actions with so high an intention, as to
serve God therein better than in far more important
things done with a less pure intention. Surely it
needs but to meditate upon the holy household of
Nazareth to realise this truth, while God's own
word tells us that " he who despiseth little things,
shall fall by little and little." Let your aim be to
please our dear Lord perfectly in little things, and
to attain a spirit of childlike simplicity and dependence.

One great hindrance in growing in God's Love is
self-love. It is chiefly thereby that Satan gets a
hold over us ; and all human respect, the fatal snare
of so many souls, springs from no other source.
All God's dealings with those whom He leads in the
hidden paths of the spiritual life, tend to root out
self-love; as, on the other hand, all our difficulties
and inward struggles arise from it. In proportion
as self-love and self-confidence are weakened, and
the will bowed to that of God, so will hindrances
disappear, the internal troubles and contests which
harassed the soul vanish, and it will be filled with

peace and tranquillity. But it is well to bear in
mind that as we advance in the spiritual life, our
self-love is apt to change in character, becoming
more refined and subtle, and consequently more
treacherous and harder to uproot. In truth, we can
only perceive this dangerous enemy by the help of
God's own light, which reveals the secrets of the
heart; and He only shews us our danger by degrees, giving us the means at the same time of overcoming it. Thus we seldom realise the force of
self-love until God's dealings are tearing it out of
our hearts; and then if we co-operate with His
grace, His love will speedily fill the vacant place,
until by degrees the whole soul is His only. Then,
indeed, that soul realises the promised blessing of
the " pure in heart"—and "shall see God." Such
a soul may suffer, but it will suffer joyfully, unre-
sistingly, and no sufferings can take away that peace
of which Jesus said, " My peace I give you: not
as the world giveth, give I unto you."

It will be profitable to review the various degrees
of the spiritual life, and to trace how God deals
with our self-love in each. Of course the most
obvious form is a sensual love of self, and a clinging to sensible and material pleasures. God draws
His servants from these by filling them with

heavenly delights and consolations, beside which earthly enjoyments grow pale and worthless. Next, self-love cleaves to these very consolations, this tangible delight and satisfaction, and then God gently withdraws external delight, without depriving the soul of peace and restfulness. But when self-love begins to rely upon this peace, then again He permits that to be troubled, and the soul loses all self-resource, all self-confidence. At times too the devil tempts the struggling soul with impure thoughts or lurking doubts; under the pressure of which it is hard to believe that we are not consenting to the evil one. It may be that the strength of such temptations increases, while we seem to ourselves capable of less and less resistance; we are aghast at the sight of our own sinfulness, and imagine that God must reject us; self-love finds no rest for the sole of its foot, and scarce knows how to serve God for Himself only, while so devoid of all tangible comfort. This condition will last probably until the soul learns not to think of itself, but to dwell in God alone; and then, indeed, self-love is conquered. God grants a new and heavenly life to the soul which has thus died to self—it is filled with Him, united to· Him. It loves, and is loved again—no more trouble, no more fearfulness, no

more temptation. Even suffering is but a fresh
stimulant to love. Such a Christian waits peace-
fully for death, which will but fill up the measure of
perfect love. " Old things have passed away, and
all things become new."

As the soul advances in holiness, God's active
power within it increases, while its own action
diminishes. It is our part to still our natural restlessness, and give place to His uninterrupted workings ; so that day by day our souls may lie more
passively in His Hand, until our will be wholly
merged in His Will. It must be our chief aim,
having given ourselves wholly to God, to let Him
take possession of all that is in us. He is
wont to take all that we give Him, even our very
moral being and free will ; yet He does but accept
the offering in order to restore it to us perfected
beyond all that the heart of man can conceive.
Even as an earthly parent might test and try the
love of a favourite child, by seeming harshness,
and then finding it unchangeable, would redouble
his tenderness and affection, so does God deal with
His children. Self-interested, calculating love, is
not the " perfect love" which alone is worthy of
God. That love knows neither limit or measure,
human prudence cannot restrain it, it reaches out to

"the foolishness of the cross." That was the love wherewith Jesus loved us: and be sure that whatever we lose in this life for His Sake, we shall win for all eternity; but what we deny Him here, will be lost to us for ever hereafter.

True Devotion

BY "devotion," I mean a soul devoted to God, and there can be no stronger form of expressing perfect readiness to bear and do all things for Him to Whom we devote ourselves. All earthly devotion (I speak only of such as is lawful and permitted of God) necessarily is limited; but there is no possible limit to our devotion to God: the moment that a shadow of reserve or hesitation slips in, it ceases to be true self-devotion.

Real devotion, then, consists in perfect readiness to do and suffer all things without exception or reserve for God's Sake, and it is indeed a most choice gift of the Holy Spirit, one which we cannot pray for too earnestly; and which we must never suppose ourselves to have sufficiently attained, inasmuch as we ought to keep up a perpetual growth in the gift itself, as in its fruits.

Such devotion is inward, influencing the very

depths of the soul, its intention and will. It does
not depend upon reason, imagination, or feeling,
nor is its existence proved by a capacity for talking
eloquently about divine things, or glowing thoughts
of God, or even by sensitiveness and tears. Devotion is not a passing emotion—it is a fixed, enduring habit of mind, permeating the whole life, and
shaping every action. It rests upon a conviction
that God is the Sole Source of Holiness, and that
our part is to lean upon Him and be absolutely
guided and governed by Him ; and it necessitates
an abiding hold on Him, a perpetual habit of
listening for His Voice within the heart, as of readiness to obey the dictates of that Voice. Thus it is
impossible to attain true devotion without an interior and recollected spirit, which is ever seeking to
possess itself in peace ; and those who give way to
the things of sense, imagination or passion, even in
that which is lawful, will never acquire that devotion whose first work is absolute mastery over the
senses, the passions and the mind. If you will look
at devotion from this point of view, you will see
that he who is inquisitive, restless, busy about other
men's affairs ; or given to criticise and discuss his
neighbours, gossiping, ill-natured, slanderous, con-
temptuous, proud and sensitive ; or self-satisfied,

opinionated, the slave of human respect, and consequently irresolute, weak and changeable—such a man, I say, cannot be devout in the true sense of the word.

He who is truly devout is much given to prayer, delighting in communion with God, and ever realising His Presence—by which I do not mean that he is always consciously thinking of God, an impossibility here on earth,—but his heart will always be united to God, and all his actions will be regulated by God's Holy Spirit. In meditation, he is not dependent upon books or methods, or intellectual efforts, scarcely even those of the will : his soul need only look within, and there is God—and God's peace. At times he may feel spiritual dryness, but that peace will always be real and blessed notwithstanding. He will rejoice more in prayer which has its measure of suffering, and wherein self-love finds no resting-place, than in such as is merely an indulgence to the imagination. Such a man never seeks himself in serving God, realizing the precept of the " Imitation"—" Wherever you find yourself, renounce yourself." He will strive to fulfil all the duties of the state of life to which it has pleased God to call him, perfectly ; as well as all the just claims of society. Faithful to his religious exercises, he is not their slave—he can interrupt, postpone, or even forsake them for a while, if need be. So long as he is not seeking his own will, he feels satisfied that he is doing God's Will. He does not seek restlessly after good works, but does what his hand findeth to do, with all his might ; and when he has done his very best, he is content to leave results with God. He prefers hidden good works to those that are seen and praised of men, but neither does he shun those where God's Glory and his neighbour's welfare is concerned.

The really devout man does not overwhelm himself with vocal prayers and religious exercises, which leave him no breathing space. He aims at constant freedom of heart. He is neither scrupulous or over-anxious, but moves on his daily road in simplicity and confidence. He is firmly set to refuse nothing God asks of him, to yield in no way to self-love ; never to be guilty of any deliberate fault; but at the same time he does not torment and worry himself with petty vexations. If he falls into some error, he does not fret over it, but rising up with a humble spirit, he goes on his way anew rejoicing. He is never surprised at his own weakness and imperfection, neither is he discouraged by them—knowing that of himself he can do nothing, through God's help, everything :—he does not trust in his own good intentions and resolutions, but solely in God's Grace and Goodness. Were he to fall a hundred times in the day, he would not despair— he would rather cry out lovingly to God, appealing to His tender pity. The really devout man has a horror of evil, but he has a still greater love of that which is good ; he is more set on doing what is right, than avoiding what is wrong. Generous, large-hearted, he is not afraid of danger in serving God, and would rather run the risk of doing His Will imperfectly than not strive to serve Him lest he fail in the attempt. The outer life of such a man should be thoroughly attractive to others. He would be simple, honest, straightforward, unpretending, gentle, kindly :—his conversation cheerful and sensible, he would be ready to share in all blameless mirth, indulgent to all save sin.

Be certain that true devotion is never gloomy either in itself, or as regards others. How should he who is in possession of real happiness, be sad ? Earthly passions,—ambition, avarice, lust, these may well make a man gloomy and absorbed, and drive him into wild mirth in the vain hope of stifling his pain. But he who truly serves God will find that His service "is perfect freedom," come what may—poverty, contempt, or pain. We still daily prove the truth of St. Augustine's well-known words, —"Thou hast made us for Thyself, and our heart knoweth no rest until it attain to Thee."

True Holiness

BUT few, even of those who have specially devoted their lives to God, have accurate ideas as to the character of true holiness. Most people believe that it consists in a routine of religious practices, and a diligent observance of certain externals. If, moreover, they occasionally experience some conscious religious emotions, they make no question but they are really holy,—never stopping to ascertain whether these emotions are from God, or merely the action of their own hearts. Yet often such persons are liable to many faults unperceived by themselves, and which it would not be easy to make them see. They may be narrow-minded, pharisaically precise in their devotions, full of self-esteem, touchy, self-conceited, obstinate, unyielding or affected in outward manner,—altogether deficient in truthfulness, simplicity, and reality. They secretly esteem themselves more highly than other men, and they may even despise and con-

demn the true piety of others, which they are unable to perceive. This unreal, harsh judgment is
sadly too common among Christians ; but surely it
is the self-same spirit which crucified our Lord
Jesus Christ; and in truth it crucifies Him in His
servants even to this day ; for whoever gives himself wholly to God, and seeks earnestly to lead an
interior life, runs a risk of drawing down jealousy
and criticism, perhaps calumny and persecution,
upon himself.

If you would realize perfect holiness, seek it as
set forth in Jesus Christ. He is our only Example,
and it was to give us such an example that He
took upon Him the form of man. All holiness
which is not shaped and formed upon that model,
is false and unacceptable to God,—and if it de-
ceives men, it can never deceive God, or win an
entrance into Heaven. Be it yours to study holiness with Jesus for your teacher, and be not slack
in asking Him for light and grace, that you may
learn His lesson perfectly.

Jesus "pleased not Himself" (Rom. xv. 3). He
never sought His own pleasure or gain ;—no single
deed of His was ever wrought with a view to the
praise of man, or that He might shun man's wrath.
God the Father, His Will, His Glory, were the ob-

jects of the Saviour's every movement. " I came
not to do My own Will, but the Will of Him that
sent Me." Our great Example has taught us that
holiness is inward—it does not consist in excited,
evanescent feelings, but in a deep honest conviction,
which finds vent in action;—in an entire sacrifice
of self to God, a boundless love and charity towards
men. Such was the spirit of the Saviour's life.
He fulfilled every tittle of the Law, but meanwhile
He taught by word and deed that all such observance must arise from inward love, or it is no better
than slavish obedience. He has taught us to esteem
this life as a mere pilgrimage—a passage—a time
of probation in which our love to God may be
ripened. He "minded not earthly things;"—He
taught us not to be anxious for the morrow, but to
rest wholly on His Father's good providence. Jesus
voluntarily embraced that life which men shrink
from most, and which they seldom endure save from
necessity. He did not condemn riches, but He
gave the preference to poverty : He did not condemn the distinctions of rank and position which
are in truth God's own appointment, but He taught
us that there is a choicer blessing, a greater nearness to Heaven, in a lowly condition ; and that self-
esteem, founded on high birth, wealth or power, is

a fatal snare. All irregular pleasures He has con-
demned, and while permitting us the use of certain
lawful enjoyments, He Himself abstained even from
these. Prayer, and the exercise of His gracious
Ministry, filled His earthly life—" Wist ye not that
I must be about My Father's business ?"

If we may say it reverently, nothing could be
more simple, even, or unaffected than the deeds and
words of our Lord. He taught "as one having
authority ;" but it was lovingly, in a familiar way,
without pomp or display ; His miracles were often
almost secret, and His apostles and evangelists
were led by the Holy Spirit to record His earthly
history with the same striking simplicity.

Remember too His tender compassion for all true
penitents—" I came to call, not the righteous, but
sinners to repentance." Think of His pitiful goodness to the publican, to Mary Magdalene, to the
Samaritan, to the woman taken in adultery ; and
compare it with His condemnation of the Pharisees'
pride, their avarice and hypocrisy. Remember too
how patiently He bore with the roughness and
frailties of His own apostles. From our point of
view, it seems as though it must have been a sore
trial to His incomparable refinement to live with
those ignorant men, full of imperfections and faults

B

as they were. Even the holiest men find no small
difficulty in sanctifying their intercourse with their
fellow creatures ;—the closer they are to God, the
more gentleness, patience, and toleration they need
in their dealings with those around—it is a perpetual
struggle. But Jesus bore every persecution in
patience, meeting every attack with truth and innocence ; silent before His accusers, forgiving His
murderers; shedding His blood for them. All who
"seek to live a godly life, must suffer persecution"
—it may be through ridicule and slander, or more
overt acts. Then is the time to take Jesus as an
example—to bear all things in defence of the truth;
to make no answer to calumny, save by a holy life;
to be silent when words are not necessary ; to leave
our justification with God ; to put aside all bitterness, all resentment; to render good for evil; to pray
for those who injure us, and believe that they are
but instruments working out God's Will upon us.
Such conduct as this is worthy to be called holy,
and God seldom sends such trials until a man has
been long proved and moulded. Blessed are they
who endure ! "If ye suffer with Him, ye shall also
reign with Him." It can only be through an altogether extraordinary grace that we could accept
such trials gladly, still less desire them. Let us

rather be content with our "day of small things,"
seeking nothing lofty for our weak purposes, but
daily imploring God that no human respect may
ever make us unfaithful to the duty which we owe
to Him.

How to attain Real and Stedfast Virtue

THE first means, which albeit seemingly the most ordinary, is in truth the hardest, is to will it. But the will must be sincere, hearty, effectual, and persevering; and such a will is no common thing. We deceive ourselves into thinking we have it, while really we have only vague wishes and desires; which are widely different from a firm resolute will. People wish to be religious, but after their own fashion—to a certain point— they would not "go too far,"—or give up anything for it; and thus they stop short in wishes. Practical religion is another thing, and they lose heart directly that any effort is required, when faults must be overcome, natural inclinations or imperfections resisted. There may be a fervent beginning, but such persons soon grow slack, they give up what was scarcely begun, and shut their eyes to the fact that everything depends on perseverance. Do you ask God daily to confirm and strengthen your will, and each day's perseverance will help forward the morrow.

The second means for attaining a stedfast progress in holiness, is to have a daily rule, and to observe it punctually.   But it is not well to overload one's self with observances at first—it is better to increase spiritual exercises gradually.   Due regard must be had to health, age, position, and the duties entailed thereby.   Be sure it is a mistaken devotion which interferes with the duties of your natural state of life.

A third means is the continual recollection of God's Presence ; and to this end you must firmly believe that God dwells within our hearts, and that He is to be found there by those who seek Him ; that He inspires us with holy thoughts, leading us from sin to seek righteousness.   What we often call conscience is in truth God's own Voice ; warning, rebuking, enlightening, directing the soul ;—our part is to be attentive in listening, and stedfast in obeying this voice.   Dissipation and excitement hinder us from hearing it ; it is when we are calm and still—our passions and imagination at rest— that the Voice of God fills the heart ; and there is no step towards perfection so great, as when we learn the habit of always watching for it.   But for this we require a tranquil heart, avoiding whatever disturbs, engrosses, or distracts it ;—and all this is the work of time, with diligent self-examination and resolute efforts.

The fourth means is to give a fixed daily time to God, during which His Presence is our sole occupation, and in which we listen to Him and talk with Him, not with the lips, but in the heart. This is real mental prayer. Those who are beginners in this exercise cannot do better than use the "Imitation of Christ," pausing on each sentence and meditating upon it. At first a quarter of an hour morning and evening is enough, but you should acquire the habit of at least half an hour's morning meditation. When you learn to take delight in it, and can dispense with the help of books, it is well at times merely to lie passive before your Lord, asking Him to work His own good pleasure in your soul : —it is a great mistake to fancy such time to be lost, whether you are so conscious of His grace operating within you or not.

The fifth means of progress is diligently to frequent the Sacraments; chief channels of God's grace. Do not make a torture of confession ;— that is not acceptable to God any more than when it is perverted into a mere formal routine—the danger to some who confess frequently. Those who aim at perfection should chiefly accuse themselves of their resistance to grace — their indulgence of self-love—their voluntary and deliberate words or deeds contrary to that aim. That Communion is unquestionably good, from which you come filled with fresh courage, and a renewed purpose of hearty faithfulness to God. Do not fancy that it is necessary to good confession or communion, to be fettered by the acts of devotion you find in books :—such acts are useful for young persons whose attention is wandering, for those who communicate but rarely, and for all who have not the habit of recollection. But those who are accustomed to practise mental prayer, will often receive, or assist at the sacraments more devoutly without the help of books.

A sixth means of progress is spiritual reading, for which a wide field is open to you. It is well to select such books as touch your heart, and rouse it to fervour. Rodriguez on Perfection is a useful book for beginners, and for those more advanced the Imitation, the works of St. Francis de Sales, Surin, and the Lives of the Saints, to say nothing of Holy Scripture above all. Your spiritual reading should in some respects be like a meditation, that is to say, you should watch for God's action within you, and pause when you feel your heart touched by what you read. ALWAYS READ WITH A VIEW TO PRACTISE. Spiritual books are not equally adapted to all minds; therefore confine yourself chiefly to those which profit you most, but avoid multiplying devotions or exercises so as to confine and hamper your mind.

The seventh means is mortification of the heart. All our natural instincts are set against our supernatural progress, and would fain subject us to self-love and sensuality; so that we must keep up a perpetual warfare both against impressions from without and corruption within. You cannot be too watchful over your heart and all its movements;—at first such watchfulness may be toilsome, but as you grow in recollection and in realisation of God's Presence, it will become easy.

An eighth means is frequent meditation on the humility and purity of the Blessed Virgin, of whom Holy Scripture tells us that she is "blessed among women." A constant remembrance of your guardian Angel, and an appeal to him for help and guidance, will also be very profitable. He is ever beside you, and his mission is to lead you on toward Heaven.

Finally, it is most important that you should be

under the guidance of a director who is himself led by God's Holy Spirit, and therefore capable of leading you in the right way. You may be certain that those who heartily desire to advance in holiness, will find a suitable guide ; God will not fail to supply their need, if they pray to Him to send them the help they require, and then receive that help with meekness and confidence. With a hearty will and wise guidance the soul can scarce fail to advance in the paths of holiness.

Victory over Self

" From the days of John the Baptist until now the Kingdom of Heaven suffereth violence, and the violent take it by storm."— MATT. xi. 11.

WHILE on the one hand our Lord Jesus made our access to Heaven easy, by the outpouring of grace and love He has given to His disciples, on the other hand, He made the path thereto more strait and narrow than before, perfecting the law and raising it to a higher standard than that of Moses. Therefore from the days of the Baptist who preached the Coming Saviour, the Kingdom of Heaven has been won through the violence done to self, and it is only by such victory that "the violent take it by storm." Hard indeed this is to nature, which must be unrelentingly thwarted, it may be even to blood. If God's service meant no more than a certain devotional routine, readily fitting in with an easy comfortable life, and with the indulgence of self-love and self-esteem, we should find more saints in the world—that is to say, more real Christians, more sincere followers of the Gospel of Christ, and our position would be a much easier one than that of the Jews, who were bound by so many external observances, from which we are exempted. But while abrogating those externals, Jesus Christ has laid upon us an internal rule which is incomparably harder to keep. "I came not to send peace, but a sword," He said (Matt. x. 34); and He bids us take up that sword and circumcise our own hearts; cutting away our corrupt affections without pity, until the old Adam perish in us.

Now this is hard to receive, hard to do. There are many persons who are ready enough to say certain prayers, go to Church, and practise some works of charity. Such religion costs little. But ask somewhat more;—the correction of faults, victory over human respect, a bridled temper, restraint of natural impulses, and the director is at once proclaimed to be severe, harsh, intolerant. Yet the gist of Christianity lies in this severity—a true Christian knows that self is his most dangerous foe, on whom he must wage perpetual war—that he is only safe when yielding in nothing to self, and that his best victory is over self. When a soul first gives itself up to God, He is wont to deal very

tenderly with it; He fills it with peace and joy; it
takes delight in solitude, recollection, and devotion
—nothing seems hard or difficult. But in a while,
when the soul is able to bear such a sight, God lays
bare its faults, He puts aside the veil which con-
cealed them, and inspires the growing Christian
with an earnest mind to overcome them. Thence-
forward the inward struggle begins;—bent upon
conquering self, the soul pursues it unrelentingly
wheresoever it is to be found, and by the help of
God's light, it is found everywhere. We see nought
save imperfection, self-seeking obstinacy, our very
devotions full of faults. We thought we loved God,
and now our love for Him seems but another form
of selfishness; we love His gifts rather than Himself; we indulge in self-satisfaction, because of those
gifts; we despise others who are less favoured. All
this God shews us gradually—did we see it all at
once, we should despair. But what we do see, is
enough to convince us that we have as yet scarcely
entered upon the path of perfection, and that many
a struggle is in store before we can hope to attain
that glorious end. The faithful soul will not despair, but rather humbly trust in God, and set forth
in His strength only, taking as its motto the precept of the Imitation: "The more holy violence

thou usest against thyself, the greater shall be thy
spiritual perfecting " (bk. I. chap. xxv. 11)—a precept breathing the very spirit of the Gospel and of
all the saints.

Violence to natural impulses of the heart, mind
and temperament—and violence which we must
ask God to direct, while we firmly resolve to do
battle with whatsoever can offend His Infinite Holiness. Henceforth we become the soldiers of Christ,
fighting beneath His standard. Hitherto He had
been only training us to the war, but now we are
come to the battle field. How long will the contest
last? So long as there is a foe to conquer; so long
as the old man, the Adam of our natural life is not
destroyed. A true Christian never lays down his
arms,—his combat is only ended with his strength ;
when that is exhausted, and he can do no more,
he remains passive in God's Hand, which henceforth
will work in him that to which human strength cannot attain. The first steps of holiness are won by
our own efforts stimulated by grace—the final ones
are wholly the work of God. Man does what he
can, but inasmuch as his work must be earthly, God
overthrows it, and substitutes His own work, leaving
man nothing save submission. We cease to act,
we suffer, because God is dealing with us ;—we no

longer do violence to ourselves, but we endure
violence, and this passive state is harder to bear,
for the soul is upheld by the consciousness of
voluntary action, in which there is always some
share of self-love and self-satisfaction. But when
God Alone acts, the soul has no power left—it sees
God working with it, but is unable to co-operate
with Him, nor can it claim any credit to itself for
His work. Thus God strips the soul of all self-
will, and asks nought of it save a willing renunciation of all the gifts and graces with which He had
endowed it, and which it fondly believed to be its
own.

This detachment is truly a hard victory, and involves the struggles of many a year. Even when
we think it is won, all may begin again, and nothing
save a supernatural courage could carry the soul
through it. My God, if this is the "violence" of
which the Gospel speaks, help me to endure it—of
myself I could not face so great trials, I should turn
away in despair, incapable of the struggle. But in
Thee Alone is my trust: "I can do all things through
Him Which strengtheneth me." Thou hast begun
the gracious work;—do Thou carry out and accomplish it. Be it mine to do that which lieth in me,
and leave the rest to Thee.

Self-sought Strength, and God's Strength

ST. PAUL said "When I am weak then am I strong" (2 Cor. xii. 10). That is, "When I am filled with a sense of my own weakness, and experiencing my utter helplessness, put all my confidence in God; then I am strong in the power of His might, then I can do all things through Christ Which strengtheneth me" (Phil. iv. 13). But on the other hand, it is no less true that when we are strong in our own conceits, we are indeed weak; when we fancy ourselves able to do and bear all things of ourselves, and glory in our strength, then is the time of utter weakness, for God withholds His support from presumption, and we are left alone.

In fact, then, our own strength is real weakness, absolute weakness, and tends to nought save humiliating falls; while conscious weakness, together with a lowly spirit of confidence in God, is true strength, God's own strength. Are you tempted to ask why God wills us to be thus conscious of our weakness? Because " His strength is made perfect in weakness;" because He is a jealous God, the Beginning and End of all that is holy; and because He would not have His creatures rely upon their own frail courage or their good intentions. When in His Mercy He leads a soul in the higher paths of sanctification, He ever begins by stripping it of all self-confidence, and to this end He allows all our own schemes to fail, our judgment to mislead us : we grope and totter, and make countless mistakes, until we learn wholly to mistrust ourselves and to put all our confidence in Him. When a beginner feels the marvellous strength of grace, and first rejoices in the clear light of God's truth, he not unnaturally fancies himself able to do and suffer all things for his Lord. Nothing seems too hard, perhaps even he craves for heavy crosses, great humiliations, honestly believing himself able to endure them. Nor is this presumption—arising as it does from inexperience and the first warm breath of grace, —displeasing to God, if the soul meanwhile be true and simple, and free from vanity and self-conceit. Nevertheless, He soon lowers all such self-confidence; let Him but hide His grace for a moment, leaving the soul to itself under the most trivial temptations, and speedily weariness and disgust come on ; difficulties unseen before spring up ; the soul fails under slight pressure ; a word, a look, suffice to disturb him who had fondly believed himself capable of so great things. Then, very likely, he falls into the opposite extreme, is discouraged and fearful, fancies that he will never achieve anything, and is tempted to cast away all his good resolutions. In truth, unless God came to the rescue, he would do so.

Such trials as these are repeated, until at length the soul fully realises its own powerlessness to do anything alone, and its need of total dependence on God. One while the trial comes in the shape of a temptation, to which we are on the point of yielding, and God upholds us when we thought all was over with us;—another time passions which we flattered ourselves were extinct, break out anew and all but overpower us; or countless lesser imperfections humble us,—we feel a strange repugnance, almost a disgust, to do what is right, our prayers and religious exercises are irksome and cold. All this is God's way of humbling us in our own conceit, and of teaching us that, without His Grace, we are capable of all evil indeed, but wholly incapable of the smallest good deed, or hope or thought. Then when, after many a fall, the soul

c

has learnt its lesson, and we are freed from all self-reliance, God gradually gives us His own strength, ever reminding us that it is not ours, but His only. And so we learn to bear sufferings, humiliations, toil, and weariness for God's Sake and the good of souls; difficulties cannot hinder us, dangers cannot appal us—and that because it is no longer we who labour and suffer, but God in us.   Such a one gives Him all the glory, believing himself to be but a frail instrument in Divine Hands.   It was in this spirit that St. Paul enumerated all his great toils and sufferings for the Gospel, adding, "I am nothing . . . not I, but the grace of God which was with me."[1] But a man must have passed through many a fiery trial, and be dead indeed to self, before he can attain to such a point.   To those who do so attain, what is left save one ceaseless song of praise ! they are one with God, He is in them, and self has ceased to exist.

How are we to approach such blessed strength ? First of all through a stedfast will to refuse nothing that God requires of us, and to do nothing deliberately which can displease Him.   Next, we must learn to take our faults humbly, as proofs of our weakness, and use them to increase our trust in God, and our mistrust of self.   We must be on our guard against

[1] 2 Cor. xii. 11 ; 1 Cor. xv. 10.

excitable feelings, and not fancy ourselves stronger or better because of them. Our true measure is what we are when deprived of sensible grace. Neither must we be discouraged at our own wretchedness, or give way to the thought that we cannot do or bear any special thing;—our duty is, while confessing that of ourselves it is impossible, to remember that God is All-Powerful, and that through Him we can do whatever He may require of us. We must learn to say with St. Augustine, "Give me what Thou commandest, and command what Thou wilt."[1] We must not marvel at our own reluctance to do right, but rather pray earnestly to overcome it, not taking credit to ourselves for any such victory —rather thanking God for it. Finally, we must equally avoid presumption and cowardice; the one springs from overweening self-confidence, the other from imperfect confidence in God. Both alike are met by the same remedy—a constant recollection that He is the Source of all strength. Who can presume who knows that his strength is in no sense his own? who despair, knowing that God, All-Powerful, All-Mighty, has promised to be his strength, and his Strong Salvation?

---

[1] "Da quod jubes, et jube quod vis." (Conf. x. 29.)

Divine Light

TURN to the 119th Psalm, and see how all
important David held God's Light to be for
the interior life. "Give me understanding, that I
may keep Thy law;" "O grant me understanding,
and I shall live;" "Shew the Light of Thy coun-
tenance upon me, and teach me Thy statutes."
In order to a full perception of our need of God's
Light, we must remember how human reason has
been darkened since Adam's fall, and that no
earthly wisdom can suffice to guide us in the hidden
paths of grace. God wills us to tread them in
faith only; and so He only gives us just such light
as we need for the present moment. It is not His
will that we should see before us, or around us, but
He never fails to grant such Light as makes it impossible for us to lose our way so long as we follow
His leading.[1]

[1]   " Did we but see,
When life first opened, how our journey lay
Between its earliest and its closing day ;

If you would indeed follow this, you must first
of all put aside all your own theories and notions
as to virtue and holiness, which are probably very
poor at best; nor must you strive to be your own
guide, and walk by the light of your own reason.
Nothing but pride and presumption will come of
that; but if you honestly give up your own will, in
obedience to God's Voice within your heart, and to
the external guidance of a wise director, you are
not likely to be deceived.

You must continually seek Divine Light, ask for
it on every occasion, great or small, undertaking
nothing without It. In the earlier stages of the interior life, it is generally very abundant; it flows in
upon you in prayer and Communion; you are surprised to find how clear the mysteries of the hidden
life seem made to you. You have an inner conviction that it is a true light, for you know that it is

Or view ourselves, as we one time shall be
Who strive for the high prize, such sight would break
The youthful spirit, though bold for Jesus' sake.

But Thou, Dear Lord!
Whilst I traced out bright scenes which were to come,
Isaac's pure blessings, and a verdant home,
Didst spare me, and withheld Thy fearful word;
Wiling me year by year, till I am found
A pilgrim pale, with Paul's sad girdle bound."—I. H. N.

in no sense your own, or the result of your own
efforts or penetration, and it has a sweet glow
which rejoices your heart.   You must receive this
passively, letting it come and go as God wills.   It
is given to do a special work at the moment ; and
when you need it again He will renew it, but He
does not choose you to claim it as a possession, or
a blessing which you can summon at will.   The
Spirit of God cannot be fettered, or subject to our
control : you must wait patiently, certain that He
will never fail you in the hour of need.

It is well to make a rule to yourself not to speak
of these lights to other men, under the pretext of
giving God glory or of enlightening them.   This
is a delusion to be resisted.   None save those whose
calling is to teach should aim at guiding their
neighbours, unless under a very distinct and special
vocation : the lights which guide you may not be
calculated to enlighten other men, whose path may
be unlike yours.   Moreover, we waste our grace by
too readily pouring it out around us.   Of course, I
do not mean but that you should do all in your
power to forward other men in the way of holiness,
but without using your personal experiences for
that end.

We need great caution in making a right use of

Divine light, and a great deal of self-mortification; neither ought we hastily to conclude that all light is of God. St. Paul tells us that Satan can be "transformed into an angel of light,"[1] and he is ever ready to meddle with all that merely stimulates the imagination, while grace influences the will and the understanding. Thus there is a danger of being deceived as to inward calls and drawings, or inspirations; and if you would avoid the devil's snares, leave the decision as to a right use of any such things to your confessor.

In order to a right use of Divine light, you must avoid, as far as may be, giving way to imagination and your own opinion, mistrusting your reason and judgment. God usually communicates Himself sparingly to people who are always reasoning and judging for themselves. The best use of reason in spiritual matters is to offer it silently at the foot of the Cross. God makes Himself known chiefly to those who are lowly and child-like in heart. He cares nothing for profound learning, or brilliant talents, save inasmuch as they are sanctified by being offered to Him. He would have us put aside all human knowledge, confessing that we know nought save through Him. The greatest saints

[1] 2 Cor. xi. 14.

have ever sought God in the spirit of little children, while many of us, in our weak arrogance, think ourselves capable of judging God's ways of dealing with souls!

"As the heavens are higher than the earth, so are My ways higher than your ways, and My thoughts than your thoughts, saith the Lord."[1] How, then, dare we presume to trust in our spiritual perceptions? How can we fail to prostrate our minds before God? as David says, "I opened my mouth, and drew in my breath, for Thy word goeth forth, it giveth light and understanding to the simple."[2] All worship involves a perpetual confession that He is the Light and the Truth—we all darkness and falsehood. Believing this, we can scarce go wrong. Let us say then with David, "I am Thy servant, O grant me understanding, that I may know Thy testimonies."[3] I cannot keep Thy law unless I know it, neither can I know it unless Thou grant me understanding. Who save Thyself can teach me how to fulfil it, either towards Thee or towards my neighbour? "Give me understanding, and I shall live."

[1] Isa. lv. 9.   [2] Psa. cxix. 30, 31.   [3] Psa. cxix. 125.

What God asks of us, and what we should ask of God

THIS is a most necessary point to ascertain in the spiritual life. For want of a clear understanding of what God expects from us, and what He allows us to expect of Him, many grievous doubts and perplexities arise, needless discontent or unjustifiable satisfaction with self, murmurs against God, even despair. Now, one thing is clear; God expects nothing from us save that which is in our power—and that is reduced to a single thing—*i.e.* a right use of free-will, as guided by enlightening grace. First, then, subject to this definition, He requires us to give good heed to the action of our own heart, and to His Voice speaking therein ; nor is this attention hard to those who love God and wish to please Him. He requires that we should not give ourselves up to anything which is calculated to distract this attention—whether it be amusement, curiosity, useless speculations, or volun-

tary excitement; and so soon as we are conscious
of any such distraction, He requires us to put away
the cause. But do not fall into the mistake of supposing that the duties of your position, or your
family, the claims of social life, or any other providential ties, need necessarily hinder this inward
recollection; habit will make it part of yourself
amid all outer claims.

Then God requires a full, hearty correspondence
with such grace as He supplies under our present
circumstances. Grace varies with varying needs.
The beginner's grace is different from that of an advanced Christian; and his again is not the same as
that granted to one far on in the path of perfection.
Mental conditions and external practices which are
suitable to one state of the spiritual life are not
suitable to another, and we must learn to accept or
quit them readily, according to the dictates of
grace. Neither must we seek after things which
are above our present capabilities, or strive to do
what may be all very well for saints, proved and
formed by God, but is all too much for our weakness.

Moreover, when once we have given ourselves to
God, He requires of us never to recall the gift, never
to act as though we were not His; always to con-

sult Him, or those who represent Him to us; to be
passive under whatever He lays upon us, and not
to strive to cast aside His chastening Hand, under
the plea that we cannot bear so great a trial. He
requires of us never to fret under the temptation,
humiliation or inward trial with which He is purifying us, but rather to ask courage to bear it to the
end.

Above all, He requires self-renunciation in all
things and for ever. But, inasmuch as there are
many degrees of renunciation, which rise in intensity
until the soul loses itself in God, our safest course
is to maintain a general resolution of sacrificing
whatever He may ask, without forecasting and
imagining all sorts of things which may never
happen. This is useless, because we cannot foresee
the future, or tell what might be our material or
spiritual attitude under such imaginary circumstances; and dangerous, because it exposes us to
the risk of presumption or discouragement. True
self-renunciation leaves all the future to God, and
only seeks to do its duty at the present moment.

God does not require sensible devotion of us, or
any of those glowing religious emotions which are
too often a subtle food to self-love. All such gifts
are His alone, He can give and recall them as He

sees fit: therefore do not be troubled when you are
dry, dull, unable to rouse yourself to any holy
thoughts in prayer or communion—still less must
you fancy that such prayers and communion are
worthless. Self-love may pronounce them to be so,
but God judges otherwise. He does not require us
to have so absolute a control over our imagination
as wholly to rule our thoughts. That is beyond our
power, but it is within our power not to dwell upon
distracting thoughts, to turn from them, to submit
to spiritual advice. It is within our power to resist
thoughts which militate against purity, faith or
hope. These are temptations which God permits
for our ultimate gain. We may ask with St. Paul to
be delivered from them ; but if the answer should
be, " My grace is sufficient for thee," we must bear
them meekly, resisting their assaults with the help
of such means as obedience furnishes.

Again, in all events which depend upon external
causes—His Providence or other men's will—God
requires us to submit, and turn them as best we
may to His Glory and our own Sanctification, per-
suaded, as St. Paul says, "that all things work together for good to them that love God." And it is
well to remember that even, in the holiest undertakings, what God requires of us is earnest, willing

labour, and the use of such means as we can command ; but He does not require *success* of us : that
depends solely upon Himself, and sometimes in very
love for us He refuses to crown our best intentions
with success.

Such, generally speaking, is what God requires of
us, and what depends upon our own free-will. As
to what we should ask of God, be sure that we know
not what we need, and that our safest course is to
leave it to Him—asking such good things as faith
teaches us to seek, and seeking to preserve a holy
indifference as to all that does not concern our spiritual progress. Above all, we must ask a true knowledge of God and of ourselves ; what He is and what .
we are ; what He has done for us and what we
have done to offend Him ; His claims upon us, the
blessing of His Grace, and the importance of rightly
using it. Then we should ask perfect confidence in
Him, so that we may say with Job, " Though He
slay me, yet will I trust in Him." We must ask to
love and serve Him unselfishly, for His sole Glory;
to believe in Him unquestioning, undoubting,
through whatever darkness or trial may come upon
us. And we should ask for such a spirit of
obedience as may wholly set aside our own will
and judgment, overrule our tastes and opinions,

and the light of our own reason, ever remembering that God's ways are not as man's ways, and
that if we would win entrance into His Eternal
Life, it must be through a total abnegation of self
and everything appertaining thereto.

God's Dealings with the Soul

"Behold I stand at the door and knock: if any man hear My Voice, and open the door, I will come into him, and will sup with him, and he with Me."—REV. iii. 20.

DURING our whole earthly life, God's unfailing desire is to "come in" to our heart, and reign there: not for His Own Sake—what need of us has He for that?—but that we may be happy, not only hereafter, but in this life. Faith, experience, reason, all prove to us, that there is no true happiness to be found for man save in God. Now, in order that we may attain this happiness, He stands for ever at the heart's door, knocking by means of holy thoughts, grateful gleams of light, pricks of conscience. If you will but look within your heart, and give heed, you will find that He is perpetually knocking thus, and that if you do not hear Him, it is your own fault. All your life long He knocks, with unwearied patience, bearing with all your slights, your resistance, your perverseness. O dear Lord, help me to recall

Thy ceaseless knocking at my heart, and my faith-
less rebellion.   Every day through all my life Thou
hast stood there, calling to me, and how often, alas !
have I refused to hearken !

But when at last the door is opened, He enters,
He takes sole possession, and nothing save our
own determination to banish Him can drive Him
thence.   Lovingly He enters, ready to fill the faithful soul with the abundance of His grace—forgiving
all the past, imparting His own Peace.   If some
souls do not experience this, it is that they have
opened the door of their heart more through fear
than love, and as yet they are restrained and cold.
Such men are liable to fall away, and their lives
are often a succession of failures and penitence.
But to those who give themselves unreservedly to
God, whose hearts are more alive to His Love than
to self-interest, His approach is full of exquisite,
unfailing joy.

Yet these firstfruits of peace are nothing as compared with that which our Dear Lord promises,
even in this life, to those who continue stedfast in
His Love.   The aim of a spiritual life is perfect
oneness with God—it is something more than union
only,—it is a very transformation—unity—like (we
should not dare to suggest such a likeness of our-

selves) that of the Ever-Blessed Trinity: "That
they may be in Us, as Thou Father art in Me, and
I in Thee."[1]   Or, again, the close intimate intercourse expressed in the words, "I will sup with
him, and he with Me;"—I will feed him with
Divine food, he shall live the very life of God.
But who is sufficient to speak of such ineffable
mysteries? We can but marvel and adore.

Let us remember, moreover, that he who would
reign with Jesus must first suffer with Him;—he
must first die to self, and to all the sensitiveness of
self-love. All the manifold trials with which God
visits us are with a view to this perfect purification of
the soul. Such trials are needful—for in no other
way can we cast aside self;—but they are hard to
bear—unbearable, indeed, unless we give ourselves
up passively to God, Who will sustain us. Such
trials are more profitable to God's glory and the
soul's salvation than the longest life of good works
and religious exercises.

[1] John xvii. 21.

D

The New Life in Jesus Christ

ST. PAUL continually reminded his converts that in Baptism they were buried with Christ, and rose again in the likeness of His Resurrection. We, too, are "planted into the likeness of His Death;" our hope and aim is that we shall enter into the grace of that His Glorious Resurrection. But to that end, we must be conformed to His Death, which was in truth only consummated on the Cross. His whole earthly sojourn was a mystical death. In like manner our new life in Jesus Christ must be a continual death to self; a dying daily to all sins and imperfections, to the world and its attractions, to the senses and bodily indulgences, to our natural disposition and besetting faults, to all self-will, to self-love or high esteem of self, even to spiritual consolations, to certainty as to our soul's condition, and to all that we can call our own in the highest matters of religion. It is as we advance in such death to all this side the grave, that the hidden life of Christ springs up and grows in us ; and when the last step is won, He raises up the soul and imparts to it, even in this world, the glories of His Resurrection.

We must die to all sins and imperfections, however seemingly trivial. The first resolve of one who gives himself wholly to God must be never to give way deliberately to any fault whatever; never to act in defiance of conscience, never to refuse anything God requires, never to say of anything, It is too small for God to heed. Such a resolution as this is an essential foundation in the spiritual life : I do not mean but that in spite of it we shall fall into inadvertencies, infirmities, errors ; but we shall rise up and go on anew from such faults— because they are involuntary, the will has not consented to them. Again, we must die to the world and its attractions ; that is, we must neither love or seek it, giving no more to it than what is required by the state of life to which it has pleased God to call us, and that as a duty rather than a pleasure. We must not stand in awe of the world's opinions and judgments, nor fear its slights, its contempt, or even its ill usage ; we must not be ashamed of fulfilling our appointed duties or of obeying Christ's Gospel, or shrink from fully acknowledging God's Law and that of conscience, because of anything the world may say or think of us. Depend upon it, in our times, none can fail to encounter many a struggle, many a hindrance, many a worldly custom to be set aside, many a worldly prejudice to be resisted, before we can hope to conquer that great enemy, human respect. This is a point on which you must examine yourself closely and unsparingly.

Death to the senses and excessive bodily indulgence. This involves watchfulness against love of ease and comfort, a restricted use of what is superfluous in food, dress, sleep; such mortifications as may be advised by your Confessor; above all, a check upon the unrestrained liberty we often give to our eyes and ears, and upon whatever tends to undue excitement.

Death to our natural disposition and besetting faults. It is no small enterprise to overcome these, and many a saint of God has not achieved the task ere he is called from this world. Every good man is not an Augustine or a François de Sales, in whom grace triumphed utterly over nature. But the best way to set forward this work is to keep watch over the heart, checking its unruly motives as they rise ; never to act or speak from impulses, temper or irritation, and always to strive after a calm self-possession.[1]   Why not do that for God's Sake which so many accomplish in the world for mere human respect?

Death to all self-will.   This covers a large field, and is a hard matter.   First of all, you must begin by subjecting your mind and will to the dictates of reason, not giving way to fancy or caprice; not being obstinate in your own opinion, giving heed to others, and yielding when they seem to be right; ready to do as they wish in matters indifferent. Then, in spiritual things, you must accept what God gives, and remain where He places you, without wishing for anything different; you must not criticise the workings of God's Grace; you must subject your will and judgment to your director; your active mind must be restrained; you must refrain from self-dissection and perpetual reasonings about yourself, seeking rather Divine Guidance; you must avoid merely intellectual reading (in the matter of spiritual books), aiming more to feed your soul than to satisfy a restless curiosity, which often leads to errors and delusions.   Strive

---

[1] Thus a holy man writes to one of his spiritual children (a religious novice), "If you can learn to walk slowly and speak slowly, I shall have hopes of you."

to remember that God will give you exactly the light you need, and be satisfied therewith. If your heart and mind are cumbered with unnecessary, self-sought rubbish, what room is there for God to come in and fill them with His Peace?

Death to self-love and self-esteem. This touches us very closely, for if there is one thing more deeply rooted in us than another, it is pride and self-conceit. They are God's bitterest enemies, and consequently ours also. He is for ever resisting and uprooting them in the soul that gives itself to Him. Be it ours to let Him deal with us, co-operating as we may.

Death to spiritual consolations. There comes a time when God weans the soul from these; we cease to take conscious pleasure in spiritual things, everything becomes tiresome, weary—we cannot realise God's Presence—we do not appreciate our own peace, and fancy we have lost it. Then the soul must freely accept all such privation, and learn to serve God for His own Sake, not for His consolations. But inevitably such service costs the natural man no light struggle—nature resists, murmurs, despairs; never mind, go bravely on, heedless of your natural reluctance to suffer.

Death to outward helps and to all certainty as to

your soul's condition. Amid all your temptations and struggles, if you find a resting-place within, or can lean upon your director, not feeling yourself forsaken of God, you will easily go through great trials. But if you have no such comfort, if you feel as though God hid His Face from you, as though you were lost to all hope, then indeed it requires a heroic courage to persevere, and say, God's will be done.

Death to all we can call our own in holy things. Perhaps you have appropriated God's gifts, and rejoice in them as though they were your own. But God strips you of them—not really, but to outward appearance, and you are no longer conscious of any grace or good, natural or supernatural. You know not what you are, or were, or will be—you can see nothing save sin, hollowness, judgment. When you have accepted this in meek submission, your mystical death is attained—and then will follow resurrection and life. But these are God's own mysteries. Let us not presume to do more than fall down and worship Him.

The Gifts of God

OUR spiritual life is, so to say, a perpetual barter with God; He gives to receive again. And so it is with the soul; but the first and last gifts are ever His—Grace during this life, glory in the life to come. And in both these God communicates somewhat of His Very Self to us. The soul in return gives itself to God—its will, its longings, its inclinations; all that is in it is wholly offered up to God in this life: in the next there will be no giving, we shall be His infinitely, inconceivably. The only time then over which we have any control is in this present life, and it is now that we must strive to co-operate with our Dear Lord's grace and gifts.

He is ever the first to seek us. "Who hath first given to Him?" St. Paul asks.[1] We know that it is so in the things which concern this life, and it is no less in those which are supernatural; the root and

[1] Rom. xi. 35.

groundwork of all is God's Grace. Have we lost baptismal grace, and do we regain it in penitence? it is God who recalls us, we should never find the right road ourselves. Or, if we have retained our baptismal grace, it is but thanks to the never-failing supply of actual grace which He vouchsafes to give us. Our faith requires us to acknowledge that every supernatural action must needs be inspired and guided by grace, and that grace is never withheld save as a punishment. We, poor, weak creatures, can do nothing save obey Him faithfully, and cherish the loving gifts He gives, with adoring humility.

These gifts are solely for our benefit. God gains nothing through what He gives us, and the return He demands is for our sake, not His. Yet how often have we abused His gifts! how impossible it is for us to offer any disinterested service to God! At best we can but strive to render Him a whole hearted obedience, never imagining for one instant that we have done enough; withholding nothing from Him; not clinging unduly even to His best gifts, but resigning them patiently at His call; persevering even when the temptation to be discouraged is well nigh overpowering.

"The gifts of God are without repentance," St.

Paul says.[1] He never takes back that which He
has given, though He tenderly rebukes the soul
which has misused His gifts, and all the time He is
ready to pour forth fresh graces if it will return to
Him. So it was with David and St. Peter, so it
ever is with all who come to Him in penitential
love. But then we must give ourselves irrevocably
to Him, there must be no drawing back, no shrinking, no regret; rather an ever pressing forward,
eager desire to give Him more and more, until
there is nothing left to give. What matter whether
we are conscious or not that God accepts our offering? Grant that He seems to ignore it. Nevertheless, we know that He would have us make it,
and that He is worthy of all and more than we can
offer. We may forsake Him, but He never for-
sakes us—His weak child wanders from Him, but
God seeks him out, and lovingly reclaims him—the
Lord's patience fails not, to the end His grace
pleads with the soul. But, alas! it is not so with
us. I know that God will never forsake me, I am
certain of His grace, but I cannot count upon my
own stedfastness for one moment? My will is ever
frail and uncertain; to-day I pledge myself never
to forsake my Master, to-morrow I wander from

[1] Rom. xi. 35.

His side. Surely this consciousness ought to arouse a deep self-mistrust, and quicken the earnest effort to persevere in rightly using every grace. Who can foresee the consequences of a voluntary neglect of any the most seemingly trifling grace; God's possible withdrawal of favour, and my own increased weakness? Dear Lord, uphold Thou me, through all my endless perils of inadvertent, impetuous faults, and through all my natural frailty. May I never for one instant offend Thee deliberately, or reject Thy grace, or withhold whatsoever Thou askest of me. How can I but fear my own weak self? do Thou rule and guide me in all things. May I be faithful to Thee through all and in all, and cleaving to Thee with stedfast purpose, may I be carried through all the storms of this life, and rest with Thee for ever at last.

A Childlike Spirit

THE first step towards the inner life is to attain a childlike spirit in Heavenly things. Our Saviour told His disciples that "except ye become as little children, ye shall not enter into the Kingdom of Heaven," and again He said that "of such is the Kingdom of Heaven." But this childlike spirit is not to be understood save by experience — it is solely God's gift, and no effort of the intellect or will can produce it.

A little child does not reflect or argue—he has no foresight, no prudence, no malice. Even so in spiritual childhood. God stills intellectual activity —the ceaseless whirl of reasoning and arguing with which man's heart is prone to bewilder itself—and fills it with the one simple thought of Himself. Then the soul ceases to weary itself with planning and foreseeing, giving itself up to God's Holy Spirit within, and to the teachings of His Providence without ;—laying aside all self-opinion, to be guided by Him Alone, in a state of simple loving dependence.

Again, a child knows no disguise—so soon as it is capable of any dissimulation, the childlike nature is gone. And it is the same in the spiritual order of things. He who has a childlike spirit is free from all affectation and constraint—his actions, words and manner are all perfectly natural—he means what he says—he keeps his word—he does not seek to hide his faults, or to appear other than what he really is, and he is devoid of all the reserve of pride.

A child expresses love and affection without restraint or pretence; and so the childlike soul in all simplicity pours itself out before God in unstudied heartfelt love; he knows no method in prayer save that of placing himself in God's Presence, hearkening, gazing, pouring out his treasures of love, it may be in words,—or more often in silence. Such a man loves his neighbour sincerely, heartily; without envy, criticism, contempt or deceit;—he never flatters, or uses unmeaning forms, but his courtesy is that of which Holy Scripture is the code. If it be his duty to reprove, he does it in love, and he is ever ready to do good to all men without affectation or ostentation, as in God's Sight, seeking no other reward.

A child is obedient and docile, and knows that

he cannot follow his own will. So in spiritual things a childlike spirit renounces his own will for that of God, however that may take shape. He does not seek to rule his own course, but gives himself unreservedly to be guided by the Holy Spirit, and by God's chosen minister to his soul; while in externals he willingly yields his own will to that of others, save where he knows a thing to be God's Will, and then indeed he is firm as a rock. A child has but little self-knowledge, and no self-inspection—he goes on simply as he is—and so the childlike spirit is not given to self-contemplation, but rather goes on from day to day content with such light as God gives him for the immediate necessity. He does not judge of the earnestness of his prayers or communions by the excitement of his feelings, leaving all such judgment to God, but goes on quietly through all the variations of his spiritual life. He knows that there must be wintry storms, frost and clouds;—that is to say temptations, dryness and weariness;—but he endures them patiently, and waits for brighter times. He is not for ever fretting as to his progress, or looking back to see how far he is getting on;—rather he goes steadily and quietly on, and makes all the more progress because it is unconscious. So he never gets troubled and discouraged;—if he falls he humbles himself, but gets up at once, and goes on with renewed earnestness.

A child is weak, and the consciousness of this weakness makes it mistrustful of itself, and wholly confiding in those it loves; and the childlike Christian knows himself to be utterly weak, unable to go one step aright. So he never trusts himself, but puts all his confidence in God, keeping ever near Him, stretching out his hand for help and strength in every difficulty. He takes no credit to himself for the good he may do, or the victories he may gain, knowing them to be God's. He does not esteem himself above other men, realising that were God to withdraw His Hand, he would assuredly fall into every conceivable sin, and believing that if those around had the grace given to him they would use it far better than he does. The knowledge of his own weakness prevents his marvelling at his falls; he has no wounded self-love, but in a true spirit of dependence he cries to God for help in the first moment of danger. Conscious weakness is the very principle of all his strength, and relying upon God's protection he knows no doubt or fear: he undertakes nothing alone; but where the Voice of God calls, he is ready to undertake all things, to brave all things, certain of success, come what may.

Innocence, peace and pure enjoyment are the portion of little children ;—they are happy without consciously reflecting on their happiness, all thought and care they leave to those who love them. So the childlike soul enjoys a most real unsought happiness which God Himself pours upon it, causing " all to work together for good to those that love Him." No storms can shake their foundation, no earthly troubles move it. Not that such a man is insensible to grief, but he is raised above its sharpness by his entire resignation to God's Will. This is a gift which can only be known to those who experience its sweetness, and in truth that experience is beyond all words to describe. My God, I am Thine, now, henceforth and for ever. Suffer Thy child to come to Thee, and dwell in Thy Presence, where alone is joy unspeakable, and rest and peace!

"Out of the mouth of very babes and sucklings hast Thou ordained strength."[1] Our Lord applied these words of the Psalmist to Himself, when the Pharisees were offended at the hosannas with which His entrance into Jerusalem was greeted. In that triumphant greeting the people accepted the Messiah

---

[1] Psa. viii. 2.

with a childlike spirit, not dwelling upon His poverty, or His lowliness, but receiving without question the truth that He came "in the Name of the Lord;" and thus the ignorant "perfected praise," while the proud intellectual Pharisee stood apart, blinded by prejudice and hardness of heart. And so among ourselves; the natural tendency of human reason is not to enter into the things of God ; rather to despise and reject them, and strange as the assertion may seem, this continually happens among religious people, who are often as real opponents to the true interior life, as the Pharisees, with all their high professions of sanctity, were to Jesus Christ and His Gospel.

No one truly enters into the things of God save through a childlike spirit, a spirit which tends to make its possessor feel incapable of arguing and reasoning, which fills him rather with a sense of weakness and ignorance that knows no rest save in God ; a spirit ready to believe, to trust, to obey. Such a man goes calmly onwards by the light of faith, content not to "choose or see his path;" his heart's prayer is—

> "Keep Thou my feet, I do not ask to see
> The distant scene,—one step enough for me."

Surely it was in such a spirit that St. Paul arose

E

from the earth, seeing no man, but gave himself
passively to be "led by the hand, and brought to
Damascus." Nothing is so fatal to the interior life
as conceit in our own reason and intellect; on
which we are certain to depend less and less as we
open our eyes to the true Light of Heaven. After
all, what are our greatest, keenest, most powerful
intellectual achievements compared to those of
Satan? He possesses deeper wisdom, keener intelligence, a loftier grasp of all intellectual processes
than the whole race of man combined; for when he
lost God's Grace for ever, he did not lose his intellectual capacity—a capacity, in truth, which is part
of his sentence, and does but add to his punishment. Those who have never sought to attain true
mental humility are apt to imagine it impossible for
mature and powerful minds, but in truth they have
yet to learn how it lies at the root of all our Dear
Lord's teaching, and how it has ever been the path
by which His Saints have trod. To give heart and
mind to God, so that they are ours no longer—to
do good without being conscious of it, to pray
ceaselessly and without effort, as we breathe—to love
without stopping to reflect upon our feelings—to go
ever onwards without pausing to measure our progress—such is the perfect forgetfulness of self, which

casts us upon God, as a babe rests upon its mother's breast. It is not by great deeds, long prayers, or even by heavy crosses that we may best give glory to God; self-will may taint all these, but total self-renunciation does in truth give Him all the glory.

But we cannot attain to total self-renunciation by ourselves. God Alone can extinguish the flame of self-love within us; He Alone can destroy the old natural man, and raise up within the heart that mystical life, by which "I live, yet not I, but Christ liveth in me." But to this end we must give ourselves up to His dealing without reserve. Now, it may seem paradoxical to say that no man living enjoys such perfect liberty as those who are thus absolutely led by the Spirit of God."[1] The world's liberty makes a fair show, but worldly men are more or less slaves to their passions and to human respect; and half-hearted Christians scarce know what freedom means. Every occasion of sin betrays them, every temptation overwhelms them, human respect enthrals them—they wish to do right, but evil is too strong for them—and that is scarce liberty when a man leaves the good he fain would do, for the evil he would shun. Neither are self-

[1] Rom. viii. 14.

willed people free, though they often imagine that they are—they are governed by their own restless, perverse imagination, they aspire to conscious warmth in their devotions, and failing to find it, they are apt to murmur at themselves and at God. Moreover, such persons are for the most part scrupulous, undecided, harassed ; in fact they are as much the slaves of self-will, as more worldly men are of earthly passions. The only liberty is where God has sole possession of the heart, and where it is wholly subject to His Grace—wholly subject, and yet in perfect liberty! "How can these things be!" True liberty is the perfection of human life, and true liberty does not consist in the power of doing evil, which is rather a pitiful inheritance of our fallen nature. God, who is Liberty perfected, cannot by any possibility do that which is evil— how then can man's freedom be in any such power? The more a man is led by the Spirit of God, the more he is raised to that true liberty which is God's, and if we writhe under such subjection of will, it is but owing to that proud spirit of independence by which the angels fell. When once earthly passions are chastened, self-will conquered, pride subdued, the voice of grace heard more clearly within the soul than that of nature, this subjection will cease

to be irksome; and these results never fail to be
attained by hearty generous efforts to gain the
mastery over our senses and imagination. Then,
indeed, a man attains to a most blessed independence of all save God. Free from the cruel bondage
of the world, he tastes the sweetness of untroubled
peace. Ambition, avarice, and lust cannot tempt
him; human respect, the criticism, and ridicule of
our fellow creatures cannot turn him aside from
what he knows to be right. Sorrows, crosses, and
humiliations lose their sting; he is raised above the
attractions and the threats of the world. Is not
this to be free indeed? Yet further, such a man
becomes free as regards himself; he is no longer
a victim to his own imagination, or the caprice of
his will. He is firm and resolved, his principles and
opinions are deeply rooted, and tell upon his every
action. God's Holy Spirit imparts somewhat of its
own Immutable Character to His weak creature,
and though he may be assailed by many an inward
storm, his will remains firm as the Rock of his
Salvation. All this must be learnt by experience, but be sure that those who give themselves
wholly to God, will be surprised to find, even at an
early stage, how different they are to what they
were. There is all the difference that we see be-

tween a calm, sunlit sea, and that same ocean tossing and heaving beneath wind and storm.

There is yet one more point of liberty to which the "sons of God" are led—they are free even with respect to Him.   Let Him do with them as He will, let Him try or comfort them, let Him seem to hide His Face, or visibly have them in His Holy keeping —their souls will alike be at rest.   Externally they may be tossed hither and thither; " all Thy waves and storms have gone over me ;" but there is peace within.   Their liberty lies in willing whatsoever God wills, asking nothing else, heedless of self, accepting all He offers.   "Asking nothing, refusing nothing," as was said by one who drank deeply of those life-giving waters of His Will.   To such souls nothing can come amiss, nothing can greatly move them.   Who would not long after such freedom from earth's weary thraldom, its restless pining heart-aches, its fears and hopes ; and even from the cares and anxieties of the half-hearted Christian, who seeks himself even in doing God's Will, and thereby loses the "perfect liberty, wherewith Christ had made us free !"

'Perfect Love Casteth out Fear'

GOD requires us to fear Him. Holy Scripture sets this fear before us continually. "It is a fearful thing to fall into the hands of the Living God." "The fear of the Lord is the beginning of wisdom," but it is the beginning only; Love is the fulfilment thereof. Holy fear is one of the gifts of the Spirit, whereby He would fit us to receive His more perfect gifts. Thus while we must seek to be filled with this holy fear both in body and soul, we must not be content to stop there, but continually aim at that perfect love which purifies and transforms fear into its own gracious self. If you are still unconverted, I would have you tremble before the judgments of God, I would seek to kindle the fear of His wrath within your heart;—it is the Holy Spirit's own Voice; and those who have turned from their past sins need to be upheld in the way of penitence by fear of His displeasure. Every one of us has great need to fear our proneness to sin,

through weakness and the force of bad habits ;—
such a holy fear will often be a most helpful weapon
against the temptations which beset us. But fear
must not be the governing motive of a Christian's
life ;—God would have a higher kind of service, He
has formed our hearts to be governed by love—
His first great Commandment, the one only worthy
offering we can bring Him. Love alone can draw
us from earthliness, and lead us to God. Love alone
softens, enlarges, raises, purifies the heart. The
Christian's law consists of two things, to shun that
which is evil, and to do that which is good. Now
fear may tend to the first, but it will never produce
the last result ; while love does both. Love teaches
us to " abstain from all appearance of evil," and to
aspire after perfection, regardless of difficulty and
self-sacrifice. There is no generosity in fear—a
literal abstinence from that which is forbidden
seems to satisfy its claims ; but love would always
fain have tenfold more to offer, and it counts its
very best as nought while some further sacrifice
can be made. Fear knows nothing of the tender
refinement and exquisite sensitiveness of love; but
when God vouchsafes to fill a heart therewith, it is
indeed a treasure to be jealously guarded and
cherished. When He visits us with His love we

begin to marvel how we could ever have feared
One so infinitely gracious, we rest on Him in childlike trust, we speak to Him with sacred familiarity;
—visions of dread no longer disturb us, and then
indeed fear is "cast out." Yet a certain filial fear remains—but it is not a fear of punishment; the
loving heart fears God because it would grieve to
offend so dear a Father,—to do the smallest thing
that could be ungrateful or displeasing to Him.
Such a soul fears to commit the most venial fault,
the slightest imperfection, simply because all shadow
of sin is contrary to God's Will; and there is no
armour so invulnerable to temptation as this sweet
childlike fear. It produces a ceaseless watchfulness, a host of loving precautions against the most
transient unfaithfulness;—it triumphs easily over
difficulties, bursts earthly bondage, and passes
victoriously through the snares of the world, the
flesh, and the devil, reaching forth joyously to the
One Sole Object of every effort and hope. But
slavish fear could never effect any such result.
Still more forcible is the desire to please Him we
love. The loving soul is calm and peaceful, yet it
is ever on the watch for occasions wherein to prove
its love—labour, suffering, sacrifice—all is welcome
so long as it can please its Lord. Recognising

self-will as His great enemy, love does violence to self on every side—for His dear Sake. It is thus that perfect love casteth out fear—until it learns to see nought save God;—neither shrinking from correction, or asking reward—self, in short, is lost "in a blaze of charity." If, then, one who has sincerely offered himself to God, should find himself at any time overwhelmed by a sudden fear of God's exceeding awfulness, I would say, See whether it be a trial sent by Him—and if so, bear it in a loving spirit. But if it be a temptation of the Evil One, seeking to move you to despair, then renew your acts of confidence in God, cast yourself upon Him, cleave to Him, and ask Him to enable you to turn this temptation to His greater glory, in detaching you more and more from all that is of self. Such a course will assuredly bring you peace, and draw you closer to your only Strength and Hope.

What Holiness is

UNDER the Law, God commanded His people to "be holy, for I the Lord your God am holy;"[1] and Jesus bade His disciples, "Be ye perfect even as your Father which is in Heaven is perfect." The whole motive power and aim of holiness is set before us in these words; but we cannot enter into their depths save through the light of grace, nor will anything teach us their full meaning so well as the attempt to live by them. There is a perfection of symmetry in God's holiness, and whatever is ill regulated and contrary thereto is displeasing to Him. He forgives our wanderings and inconsistencies when we repent and forsake them, but if we reject His Mercy and persist therein, He inevitably punishes them, because He is holy. He has made us in His own Likeness, and He requires us on our side to strive after the perfecting of this resemblance; He has endowed us with free-will and

1 Lev. xix. 2.

intelligence, and it is our part to aim at being holy, because He is Holy. How else dare such a wretch as I am dare to approach God ? He has made us for Himself, all I have is of Him, therefore I owe Him ceaseless gratitude ; I need Him perpetually, therefore I must ever hope for Him; I wait for His gifts, I can find no rest save in Him. But how shall I attain this blessed intercourse with my Lord, save through holiness ? An unholy soul is ever going farther and farther from Him, and He from it—and the end must be total separation from Him for ever.

Moreover, the work of Grace has drawn me still nearer to Him than that of my first creation. God has given me supernatural gifts ; He has made me with a view to an eternity spent in His Presence, and sharing His Blessedness. How tenfold then is the force of that commandment, "Be ye holy, for I am holy." How can I hope to share His bliss, to be united to Him, without holiness ? What can be so all-important to me in this life, as a growth there-in ? and how can I hope to grow in holiness save by His Grace, before whom the Saints in Paradise ever bow down with the song of praise, "Holy, Holy, Holy, Lord God of Hosts."

It was that we might attain to this holiness that

we were engrafted into the Divine Nature; "be-
gotten again unto a lively hope by the resurrection
of Jesus Christ,"[1] not joined to Him spiritually
alone, but our bodies made "the members of Christ."[2]
Who can ponder this truth, and not be filled with
an awful sense of the personal holiness required of
him as a Christian. In primitive times the Apostles,
impressed with this verity, addressed all believers
as "Saints;" but could we dare now to use such
language to Christians? Are not too many of those
whose calling is the same as that of Christ's first
followers practically enemies of His holiness? and
that while the standard set before them is God
Himself. Remember it is Christ Who said, "Be ye
perfect, as your Father which is in Heaven is perfect." Can we be holy even as He is Holy? In
truth no; but every action and thought must be
moulded, shaped upon His Example, before we can
fulfil the precept. It was to this end that God
became Incarnate, and dwelt among men—that we
might have an Example which, clothed in our
human flesh, subject to all our infirmities, we
might follow, as we cannot follow an Invisible, All
Powerful God, and our Example is likewise our
Guide and our Strength; He supplies the Grace

1 1 Pet. i. 3.   2 1 Cor. vi. 15.

whereby we may follow Him, He is continually offering it to us, and the more we claim, the more abundantly He pours it out upon us. Those who would use it rightly must do so through His strength; they must give themselves to Him, and never recall the gift; they must leave their souls in His Hand, as the clay in the potter's—"living or dying they must be His;" and He will perfect the good work He has begun in them.

He who has fully grasped the principle that God is All, and the creature nought, has mastered the whole spiritual life. Its object is to give to each that which is due; *i.e.*, to God everything without reserve; to the creature simply nothing—and therein lies perfect humility and perfect submission to Grace. He who begins to give himself heartily to God, opens his eyes to what God really is—not after a merely speculative, unprofitable fashion, but with a perception which reacts upon his whole life—internal and external. Such knowledge cannot fail to strip off the delusions of self, and as we learn to see our own utter nothingness and emptiness, we shall be more and more filled with God. So long as we think anything good of ourselves, or aim at any self-chosen path, God is not really our All in All. God is All in the natural order of things; without Him nothing is made—and the gift of existence includes all other gifts. Thus I owe whatever I am or have to God—my intellect, my memory, my will—all are of Him ; and if I use them as my own, if they move me to vanity or self-conceit, I defraud Him of His right; I cast myself practically below those I despise in my pride, I become the enemy of God. "Who maketh Thee to differ from another? and what hast thou that thou didst not receive? Now, if thou didst receive it, why dost thou glory, as if thou hadst not received it?" asks St. Paul.

Again, God has made all for Himself—all creation depends upon Him, He is the sole end of all things. In one sense undoubtedly, this world is made for man, but only that man may use the gift to God's Glory, and therefore he is bound to use those mental powers which he alone of all creation possesses, and all the external benefits he enjoys, to God's service. So soon as man holds himself to be independent, and appropriates to himself the wondrous mental faculties with which he is endowed; so soon as he uses the inferior creation with which he is surrounded other than as God's wills; so soon as he prefers the creature to the Creator, so soon he becomes a mere graceless rebel. Man ranks even lower in the order of grace than that of nature. By the order of grace this intelligent being, man, in spite of his own nothingness, is destined to the eternal possession of God—a destiny so sublime, so beyond all save supernatural grace, that nothing higher can be conceived. Unless God Himself had made known to us that such is our destiny, no human intellect could ever have attained so great knowledge; and unless He had shown us the means whereby to attain to this glorious end, we could never find the way. Our holy faith, its worship, its Sacraments, are God's appointment; human reason could not have invented them, neither has it any authority by which to institute them. Man can neither desire or seek eternal life of himself. Grace must continually co-operate with his free-will. Even without the hindrance of original sin, it must have been so—and how much more under the tendency to evil, the aversion to good which is the result of natural concupiscence? Ignorance, weakness, and passion all tend to darken man's reason; without grace he can do no good thing, and that grace is the free gift of Jesus Christ. How often, too, original sin is strengthened by years of fatal habits, unresisted temptations! What then save God's persevering grace can save His sinful child? Surely

He is all, and man nought, and worse than nought, in the matter of sanctification. This seems like a dark picture, and yet more or less it applies to us all, for how few have kept their baptismal purity? One deliberate sin, one resistance to grace, one refusal to obey God's call, may be our eternal destruction! And how easily such things happen! A moment's self-complacency, a thought of pride of our own good works, or of contempt for a fellow creature, such may be the beginning of a worse state of things than that from which God's Mercy originally saved us. Who but must tremble at the thought, who can think great things of himself if he remember what he has been, what he would be without God's help, what he may any day become, if he trusts to his own strength rather than God's upholding Hand?

F

The Blessed Virgin a Model of the Interior Life

WE shall find a valuable lesson as to the interior life in those words of Holy Scripture concerning the Blessed Virgin, "Mary kept all these things, and pondered them in her heart."[1] Let us reflect a moment upon what God did for her, and on what she offered in return to Him. He chose her out to be the Mother of Jesus Christ; He gave her high favours—"the Lord is with thee, blessed art thou among women;"[2] and He gave to her such a share as none other could ever know alike in the Cross and the glory of Christ.

In return, Mary offered to God a purity, a humility, and a submission which may be well taken as the model of an interior life. She did not reason upon God's mysterious dealings with her, incomprehensible as they were to all save the eye of faith. It is ever so in the hidden life; He leads souls by ways

[1] Luke ii. 19.   [2] Luke i. 28.

altogether contrary to human notions; He overthrows earthly judgments; He disconcerts all our
efforts, overrules all our self-conceived plans. We
have but one course to adopt, and that is to say
with Mary, "Be it unto me according to Thy word."
She aimed at no great things, her "low estate"
satisfied her, nor did she believe herself to be likely
to be chosen for the very highest honour a created
being could ever know, the mother of God. And
in the hidden life, those only can serve God truly
who realise their own poverty and helplessness, and
rejecting every proud thought, look for nothing
save His grace. Mary's share in her Son's Cross
began with His birth, and followed her to Calvary,
and beyond it. Most Christians fail to see much
further than our Dear Lord's bodily sufferings upon
the Cross, and His Mother's sorrow in beholding
them; they lose sight of the life-long expectation
of those sufferings, of the ingratitude which pierced
the Heart of Jesus when men "would not" be saved,
of the mental agonies of the Saviour, and the
sword which pierced Mary's breast.[1] Yet all the
while that she was sharing her Son's weight of
anguish, a weight which none save God might bear,
what was she externally? A poor Jewish woman,

[1] Luke ii. 35.

dwelling for thirty years at Nazareth in her homely simplicity, later on without even that lowly home, dependent on the loving charity of St. John. What stir did she ever make in the world? or when did she ever come prominently before men's gaze? What did she do externally to promote her Son's Gospel? And yet in truth she is "blessed among women," as the gracious channel whereby redemption came to sinners. In truth God's ways are not as our ways! Lowliness, obscurity, silence, are very precious in His Sight, and He is more wont to use as His chosen instruments those who affect nothing, esteem themselves as nought, and shrink from earthly applause than all others. Who can meditate on the life of our Dear Lord and His Blessed Mother, and doubt it? Lowliness, absence of self-esteem, love of an obscure life, silence, solitude, diligence in giving heed to little things, faithfulness to grace, to prayer and recollection, total submission to God's Will, complete self-sacrifice, all these are of the very essence of the true interior life, and all these we shall find more perfectly set forth in Holy Mary, as recorded in the Word of God, than in any other earthly example set before us by the Holy Spirit. "Behold Thy mother." They are our Dear Lord's own words. Let us take them in a childlike spirit, and contemplating lovingly the features of that loved and loving mother, let us pray Him to mould us more and more upon that sweet model of purity, holiness and hidden life.

Resignation

"FATHER, into Thy Hands I commend my
Spirit." It was at the moment when our
Blessed Lord's earthly anguish had reached its
climax that He thus summed up the perfect sacrifice
He had taken upon Himself, and gave utterance to
that which had been the ruling power of His Incarnate Life—total submission to His Father.
What act was ever so full of pure disinterested love!
Love cannot be separated from faith and hope,—on
the contrary, it perfects both in faithful souls.
There may be no definite conscious sense thereof,
but the reality is assuredly there; and the true
interior life, while it tends to deepen and ripen love,
confirms faith and hope at the same time. God's
Grace does indeed enable some of His favoured
saints to follow their Master in His utter self-
abandonment;—there have been souls able to re-
sign everything to God, but this is the work of
extraordinary grace, and usually the result of no

common purifying sorrows. Such a soul is ordinarily led into circumstances of special retirement, in which meditation becomes its chief occupation. One sacrifice after another is required of it ; trials and temptations, temporal and spiritual, are heaped upon it. The soul becomes unable to see its own condition clearly, and feels as though all were wrong with it, as though God had altogether forsaken it. Thus God leads His servant to the edge of what may be likened to a vast spiritual abyss, and then calls upon him unhesitatingly to plunge therein ; and thenceforth He imparts a new and glorious life to the self-forgetting soul. But all this is a mystery only to be read beneath supernatural light : and to many of us it must remain a sealed book. At all events let us respect what we cannot understand, and abstain from rash judgments, remembering that what is impossible with men is possible to God.

God repeatedly makes Himself known to us in Holy Scripture as a Jealous God—jealous of our heart and mind, requiring that we give Him, not a barren, speculative homage, but such worship as will influence every act and thought of our lives. Intellectual homage consists in acknowledging that God is All in All, the Beginning, the End of all things, and that without Him nothing is. It con-

sists in the prostration of all our faculties before
Him, of every mental power, natural and supernatural; in willing to see as He sees, to judge as
He judges; in a continual death to self-will and
self-chosen ways, to follow His Will. He exacts
this homage with jealousy, and those who refuse it
to Him, and choose to walk by their own light, are
no better than rebels. All the fatal errors in faith
and practice which distract Christendom have arisen
because men in their pride of intellect have neglected
"the True Light, which lighteth every man that
cometh into the world."[1]

The heart's homage consists in accepting God as
the source whence all affections flow, in loving Him
wholly and with all our strength, and in loving all
else in Him and subject to His Love. Such homage
is His right, whether as our Creator, our Father or
our Protector, and experience teaches every faithful
soul that there is no happiness on earth for those
whose hearts are not stayed on Him. All ill-re-
gulated love becomes the torment of the heart, but
all that of which He is the channel, fills us with an
abundant peace which this life's chances and changes
cannot destroy. God is infinitely jealous; and as
we ponder on this truth, and then on our own deeply

1 John i. 9.

rooted, subtle self-love, which we only half fathom or perceive, we may well tremble! How am I to root out this self-love, which is part of my very being? many a struggling soul cries out.

In truth no man can conquer self-love by his own efforts;—but he can give himself up simply to God; he can leave God to work the destruction of that self-love, he can second the dealings of God's loving jealousy, he can lie still under the Hand which strips and chastens him in seeming severity, Not that such submission is easily attainable ; there must be many a trial, many a struggle first, but he who perseveres, and who, having given himself to God, refrains from recalling the gift, will sooner or later be successful. God's jealous love never leaves its task unfinished, and the faithful soul may trust in Him that He will give " patience its perfect work." When self-love is uprooted, that Love is satisfied, and broods in blessing over its conquest. Heaven would be no longer Heaven if self-love could find entrance there.

Pure Love of God

PURE love is the Love of God, free from all intermixture of self; consequently any act of love, whether it springs from hope, gratitude, or reverence, is pure so long as it is free from the love of self. None save God can tell whether we love Him heartily and purely; He has seen fit to withhold any certainty as to our own mental state from us, in order that we may be humble and trustful. One thing is clear—true love and self-love cannot dwell together—which ever is strongest will uproot the other. Self-love has its root in our own interests, it keeps them ever in view. God is not its aim and end; even in spiritual things it seeks Him for its own gratification, its own advantage. In material things it tends to mortal sin; in things allowable it produces imperfections and perversions. But the love of God is altogether pure in its origin, though varying in degree and intensity. When a soul first begins to love Him truly, there will be much of self clinging to it, and God bears indulgently with this imperfection, often using it to detach us more and more from things of this world, and by slow yet advancing steps in self-renunciation, He leads us into the interior life. Little by little He purifies His weak child, one while He withdraws spiritual consolations—our prayers and communions become dry, our affections slacken, our heart seems to grow cold. Then the soul is tempted to think itself forsaken of God, and to give up all its high aims. To do this would be a proof that we were only seeking our own satisfaction in spiritual things, but the faithful soul will persevere under such dryness steadily for love of God, and so will grow in Love of Himself, as apart from His gifts.

After these beginnings, God often withdraws all conscious delight in His Love for long intervals ; the soul ceases to feel that it loves or is loved, all self-consciousness (which tends to feed self-love) is crushed, and yet in truth that soul loves more fervently than before: the creature is set aside, and God takes sole possession of the heart. Such love does not multiply formal acts, its best proof is in forgetfulness of self—it is ever reaching forward, and losing itself in God.

Purifying love works often through temptations,

which seem to us to be uprooting those very virtues
which in truth they are strengthening and confirm-
ing—purity, faith, hope, charity towards our fellow men, holiness, self-restraint. All these may
encounter fierce temptations, but they are all external to the soul, and it is not really shaken by
them. Still that fact is hidden from it; it fears
lest it has consented to temptation, and however
we may encourage it, such a soul remains fearful
that it has sinned. Thus it becomes very prostrate,
very humble in self-accusation and condemnation,
and all high thoughts, all self-esteem is thoroughly
driven forth by a true, pure love of God; which
makes the soul dread that in spite of good intentions, it is displeasing Him. Meanwhile, in truth,
that soul is as far as possible from consenting to sin,
and by a true, most beautiful contrition, it is drawing close and closer to God.

Again, purifying love works through humiliations.
One who has been highly esteemed by all around,
suddenly finds himself slandered, and sunk in the
opinion of those he looks up to. His words and
actions are misinterpreted and unkindly judged, he
is forsaken by friends, harshly blamed by those in
authority. But he is silent, he accepts such blame
as deserved, he seeks not to be justified, and God's

Love establishes yet a fresh victory over self-love in that man's heart. But what when God Himself seems to forsake him, and shows His Face only as a stern Judge? Then is the moment when suffering man attains the closest likeness to his Saviour on the Cross—he too cries out "My God, my God, why hast Thou forsaken me!" but he owns God's Power, he submits, and by this final sacrifice all earthly soils are swept away, and God reigns Alone in His servant's heart. But beware of supposing that these severe trials are incompatible with hope. It never fails amid the sharpest temptations. God and Satan are alike known by their works. Satan's first triumph is through pride, and he goes on to attack the flesh. God begins with triumphing over the flesh, and His latter victory is a complete annihilation of pride, even through the bitterness of temptation. But hope is never absent where His Hand works; to doubt it were to doubt His Grace.

The Hidden Life of the Manger

THE interior life finds its lessons in the manger no less than in the Cross; the one contains the rudiments, the other the perfection of that life, and he who would attain the height must begin at the beginning. The Incarnate Lord has shown His interior dispositions in coming upon this earth —Love of His Father, love of men. "Wherefore when He cometh into the world, He saith, sacrifice and offering Thou wouldest not, but a body hast Thou prepared me: in burnt offerings and sacrifice Thou hast had no pleasure. Then said I, Lo, I come to do Thy will, O God."[1] That will was that He should bear our sins, and God's Justice—and from His Birth Jesus accepted it, from the manger He faced the Cross, He desired it—"for this purpose came I into the world."

Now, from this we learn a great lesson, namely, that the chief feature of a hidden life is the Cross;

[1] Heb. x. 5-7.

that it is the first thing God sets before us; that
the first work of a soul which truly seeks Him is
to accept the Cross,—we mean a total setting aside
of self for God, total renunciation of our own interests for those which are His. He Alone knows
all that may be involved in this sacrifice, but we
need not doubt that He will give us courage to
accept and strength to bear whatever He requires
of us. Be it ours to give ourselves without reserve
to Him, and to say with Christ, "How am I
straitened till it be accomplished."

The first Adam entered the world a perfect man;
the second Adam chose rather to come as a little
child, that we might learn to be as babes in dependence on grace, in simplicity, in obedience. As
a Babe, Jesus adored His Father no less perfectly
than when He spent nights in prayer, or on the
Cross, but it was a silent, passive adoration, which
we should do well to remember when our pride is
wounded, because we are cold, lifeless, unable to
express ourselves in prayer. Such a mortified condition, so bitter to self-love, may be more acceptable to God than our seasons of warm, flowing
devotion. To be in silent humility before the
Presence of God is really to serve Him "in spirit
and in truth." He does not need our glowing

lights and moving imaginations, which may be feeding self-complacency more than the soul's true health; but that silent, lowly prayer which is joined in intention to the Child Jesus praying in His Manger, will bring us very near to God.

Again the Holy Spirit teaches some great lessons of the interior life from the Infant Saviour's first days on earth—from the mean stable, the poor swaddling clothes,—humiliation, suffering, neglect, the very atmosphere in which He first drew breath. Where else could we read so perfect a lesson of detachment from the good things of this world, of total contempt for earthly honours and pleasures as that which Jesus set before His followers here? And that which He chose as His first portion, He chose for all His earthly sojourn; poor, labouring with His own Hands, without a place wherein to lay His Head, unknown or despised of men, bearing all possible sufferings and persecutions to the end. Remember, too, who they were who were admitted into His Manger. None without a special, miraculous call, as though to teach us that we cannot attain to an interior life without our vocation be of God, and that those He calls must resemble the Shepherds of Galilee in lowliness and freedom from worldly longings; in vigilance, for it was during their night watch that they were called ; in faith, for had they doubted the Heavenly Vision, they would never have found Christ. Or if they be among the great ones of the earth who are called to seek an interior life, they must be like those Eastern Kings, humble in greatness, ready to leave all at God's Voice, wise without self-confidence or presumption, open to the leading of Heavenly Light, bowing before the guidance of the Star of Righteousness. God has not left His Church without some glorious examples of the interior life among crowned heads, and those crowned with the yet nobler diadem of wisdom and learning—and very sure it is, that they and all His Saints, now surrounding the Throne of the Lamb in Glory inconceivable, drank deeply at that well of lowliness which springs forth in ever fresh streams of purity and life from the cradle of our Incarnate Lord.

G

Jesus Christ the Way, the Truth and the Life

JESUS CHRIST gathered up the whole mystery of faith, hope, and love for man, when He said, " I am the Way, the Truth, and the Life." True Life, the eternal life of the soul, is our one real heart's aim, and Jesus tells us that He is that Life. Who but Himself then should be the absorbing object of our love? That Life can only be attained by forsaking all that is false and delusive, and by cleaving stedfastly to the truth ; and Jesus tells us that He is Truth Itself. Who but He can " lead us into all truth ?" How can we find this truth ? He Alone is the Way, and it was to be our guide along that narrow path that He came into the world.

His whole doctrine was summed up into two precepts—love of God and love of our neighbour. Love of God implies a rightful and true love of ourselves, inasmuch as to love Him is to love our

only true good ; but it banishes all earthly self-
love, and leads to real detachment and sacrifice.
" He that loveth his life shall lose it, and he that
hateth his life in this world shall keep it unto life
eternal."[1]   And the outline of love for our neighbour, which Jesus sets before us, is that we have
all One Father—God :—One Home—Heaven.   We
are to love our brethren because they are loved of
God and of Jesus, and we are to love them with
the same love as His—a love which bears, suffers,
forgives all things, and is ready to give even our
very life for their soul's sake.   The whole life of
Jesus teaches this even more than His words.   His
Life is the very model of detachment, renunciation,
humiliation, patience, tenderness, gentleness, and
forgiveness.   And all His faithful servants have
trodden in the same path, believing that the only
way whereby to " put on the Lord Jesus Christ,"
is to follow Him as our Way, to love Him as the
Truth, to possess Him even in this world as the
Life.   There is but One Way, One Truth, One
Life, and all who seek another, are wandering and
lost.   " There is a way that leadeth unto death,"
and there is no mid-way, be sure ; you must follow
one or the other.   Blessed are they who take Jesus

[1] John xii. 25.

for their sole guide ; the Way will be trodden and past in time, but the Truth and the Life will abide for evermore. " If we be dead with Him, we shall also live with Him : if we suffer, we shall also reign with Him : if we deny Him, He will also deny us."[1]

[1] 2 Tim. ii. 11-13.

The Mind of Christ

" Let this mind be in you, which was also in Jesus Christ."

BY the interior mind of Christ, we mean that which was the principle and rule of His Life. It is the inner mind which stamps all our actions, and which causes the wide difference between things seemingly alike, according to the purity and holiness of the motives whence they spring. Jesus is the model of all Christians, and those who would study the interior life, must seek to know what was His mind. Holy Scripture reveals much of this to us, as regards His Father, Himself, and mankind. As regards His Father, Jesus ever offered Himself as a Victim to God's Glory and Justice. From His first coming into the world, St. Paul tells us, He offered His Body as a substitute for the sacrifices of the Old Covenant. His Will was wholly subject to that of God. "My meat is to do the Will of Him that sent Me, and to finish His Work." "The zeal of Thine house hath eaten me up." "I have a baptism to be baptized with, and how am I straitened till it be accomplished !" As regards Himself, Incarnate Lord as He was, nothing could surpass His humility, His abnegation, His readiness to bear all things. " I am a worm and no man, the very scorn of men, and the outcast of the people." As regards mankind, He was all love and gentleness, all grace and mercy, full of compassion and forgiveness. His death was for all mankind, but it was also for each individual soul. "Greater love hath no man than this, that a man lay down His life for his friends ;" and He gave His for His enemies. How dare we approach such an Example of sacrifice, humility, and love ? How else save by union with God ? His union with God was Divine:—man can be but human—yet, if we heartily seek it, if we give ourselves wholly to Him, desiring only that which He desires, and leave ourselves to His dealing, we shall attain to that union. Little by little He will open our eyes to His light, we shall see as He sees, judge as He judges. He will fill us with His strength and grace. He will guide us every moment of our life, and cause "all things to work together for our good." But we cannot do this unless we renounce all self-chosen light, all love of self, all trust in our own wisdom and knowledge. " When I am weak, then am I strong." He who would leave his life in God's Hands, must wish nothing, foresee nothing, bring about nothing ; he must simply " abide in the calling wherewith God hath called him," in patient trust and obedience. All this is implied by union with God. That includes oneness with Christ, and our life will then be conformed to God, as was that of His Dear Son. To be " perfected in the Likeness of Christ !" " Behold what manner of love the Father hath bestowed upon us."

The Effects of Holy Communion

"He that eateth My Flesh and drinketh My Blood, dwelleth in Me, and I in him."—JOHN vi. 56.

OUR human intellect fails before this marvellous Indwelling;—we cannot attempt really to understand such Divine words in their full meaning. The purer the heart, so much more will the Saviour's promise be fulfilled; and as the heart grows in holiness, so will it attain to an increased knowledge of the depth of that wondrous Presence within it. But if you ask who will tell us what it is to have Jesus Christ dwelling in us, and we in Him? there is but one answer;—No created intellect can fathom the mystery;—let us not seek to analyse it, let us rather seek so to live that it may be ours. That blessed Indwelling is intense—It is a union between Jesus Christ and the soul, such as cannot be found in the natural order of things. His Body unites Itself to our body, His Soul to our soul, His Will to to our will, in a supernatural transcendental manner so that He lives in us, and we in Him—thought, feeling, action, all is penetrated by Himself. It is a universal Indwelling, from which nothing in us is excluded, save sin only. It is enduring, eternal; by the Saviour's Will—and nothing short of our wilfulness can destroy the union contracted in a communion made with right dispositions. But we must not think to measure this blessed Indwelling, by the passing warmth of sensible devotion;—the only true test is the abiding condition of the soul. If you find that your communions detach you more and more from the things of earth, if these become tasteless, wearisome to you; if you advance in earnestness of purpose and stedfastness in duty; if you live more in the spirit of a stranger and pilgrim journeying towards his Home, who only makes use of the rest and refreshment he needs by the way as a help to arrive there the sooner;—if you come from the Altar with growing recollection, increased love of prayer, truer self-denial, decreasing self-complacency and self-will; if your thoughts and feelings are becoming more conformed to the mind of Christ, so that you instinctively measure all things by that standard, recoiling from the world and its maxims, shunning what it prizes, loving that which it rejects;—if such are the result of your Communions, then indeed you have good ground for believing that they are blessed to you with the highest blessing,—that Jesus Christ "dwells in you and you in Him ;"—each Communion will perfect the likeness to your Lord, and gradually you will be "transformed into His Likeness." Thus the real way by which to gain all that which our Dear Lord promises in His Blessed Sacrament of the Altar, is to strive after each Communion to dwell more closely in Him, to give yourself up to the guidance of His Spirit, to seek His Gracious Help in every deed, word and thought. All this requires a vigorous and sustained exertion, but it should be made calmly, without restless anxiety, or self-confidence, for our own efforts only hinder us if they are in any sense independent of God's action in us. If you sincerely believe that Christ comes in Holy Communion to dwell within you, what better safety can you find than in committing all that concerns you unreservedly to Him ? So long as you are determined simply to follow Him, you will be at rest; but if you begin to be eager and anxious, you will grow self-seeking and mistrustful, and stray from beneath His guiding Hand.

There is no preparation for a good Communion so safe as that which Jesus Himself makes within the soul that abandons itself wholly to Him ; no act of thanksgiving so hearty as that with which He inspires it. What are we that we should make ourselves worthy to receive our Lord, or to give Him fitting thanks when He has vouchsafed to come to us? There is no mental attitude so profitable to our spiritual progress, so conformable to our blessed Faith, or which renders so much glory to God as that which places the soul unreservedly at the Feet of Jesus, so that He is the motive power of every thought and feeling, every word and every act. This it is when "I live, yet not I, but Christ liveth in Me."

Moreover, this wondrous Indwelling, the result of Communion in His Body and Blood is like to the Indwelling of Christ in His Father. "As I live by the Father, so he that eateth Me, even he shall live by Me."[1] The Father is the Spirit of life to His Incarnate Word, and even so the Son is the Spirit of life to those who eat His Body. It is a supernatural life which nothing save our sin can destroy.

Christian soul, let your prayer be that you may indeed be filled with that blessed Life each time that you receive the most Precious Body and Blood

[1] John vi. 57.

of Christ :—that you may filled to overflowing
therewith, and that between each Communion your
capacity for receiving it may grow and strengthen.
To that end seek to do nothing of yourself, but all
things in and through Him.   Do not fear that this
will make you slothful—we are never so active as
when God's Holy Spirit works in us.   Our own
efforts soon slacken,—His only are renewed day by
day.   But do not search too curiously even into
these, or be for ever dissecting your own fervour.
Sometimes it is most real when we are least conscious
of it.

It was that we might the better appreciate how
closely the Sacrament of the Eucharist and the
Cross are united, that our Dear Lord instituted the
former directly before His Passion.   He made
bread to be His Body, wine to be His Blood, that
Blood which was about to be poured forth upon
the Cross.   He said, "This is my Body, which is
broken for you."   "This is my Blood which is shed
for many for the remission of sins ;" thereby retain-
ing the spiritual character of a sin-offering in the
Sacrament of the Altar, and when He gave His
disciples power to consecrate His Body and Blood,
He expressly bade them do it "in remembrance of
Me ;" that is of the sacrifice of the Cross.   At the

same time He appointed this Sacrament as the
indispensable food of our souls, whereby alone the
Life of Grace should be preserved, confirmed and
increased within them.   Thus He has for ever
graven His Cross in the souls of His faithful followers by His special institution of this Sacrament
which binds them to it for ever   Do you desire to
communicate profitably, and in accordance with
His Intentions ?   Come with a special desire that
you may thereby grow in love for His Cross, that
is for humiliation and suffering, self-renunciation,
and self-oblation.   Let this be the test of your
Communions.   Do not hold them to be good, because you have been kindled with warm glowing
feelings, but rather if you have come away with
fresh courage to conquer self, to fight against your
own will, to bear whatever God may lay upon you;
if, in short, you are more able to seek God for Himself, more willing to love His corrections as well as
His favours.   You may be certain that when your
Communions produce such results, they are good,
forwarding your own soul's progress, and promoting
God's Glory.   Sometimes we are uneasy because
our Communions are without any sensible sweetness, or warmth of feeling, and because we are not
conscious of receiving any direct grace therein.

But if this is not the result of your own fault, or of
any voluntary negligence, be not disheartened ; it is
a sign that the Holy. Eucharist is rather becoming
strong meat to you, than the milk of babes.   It is
a proof of spiritual weakness when we need so
much sensible consolation ; and when we can communicate without thinking so much about ourselves,
and our conscious satisfaction, without even wishing
for tangible results in the way of consolation, it
shows that we are becoming stronger, more capable
of living the life of the Spirit, that our love of God
is being purified, and freed from self-love.   This is
a most important point to master, and make part
of your practical life.   The Body of Christ is the
food whereby our spiritual strength is sustained ; it
follows that that strength is the test how far our
Communions are profitable.   It is plain that such
strength is to be used in overcoming self, our
natural inclinations and dislikes, our sloth, our
weakness, our inconsistency, the horror we have of
all contradiction, restraint and humiliation; in short
all that resists God's Grace within us.   If this
strength increases with each Communion, if we acquire self-control, if we are less self-indulgent, more
devoted, more patient, more stedfast in our resolutions, more indifferent to the world's praise and

blame, more docile to the leadings of grace, we may rest satisfied that our Communions are good. If you are not able to judge whether all this is so in yourself, as indeed God would not have you judge, trust in your director's judgment, and do not fear to communicate as frequently as he may advise, even if you are inclined to doubt whether you gain anything by it. Satan knows well the infinite importance of frequent Communion for all progress in the interior life, and he tries every means to keep us from it. One time he fills a man with a vague fear of sacrilegious Communion;—I call it advisedly a vague fear, because it has no definite ground, and is simply imaginary. Conscience bears no special witness against you; you have not been guilty of any deliberate negligence, and yet you are troubled, and afraid lest in St. Paul's words you "eat and drink damnation" to yourself.[1] But you must put such fearfulness aside with a steady hand, and go trustfully to the Altar of God, and you will find that such fears will pass away with your Communion. Another time Satan whispers that you gain nothing from receiving the Blessed Sacrament; especially if you are being weaned from sensible affections in

1 1 Cor. xi. 29.

Holy Communion. This temptation must be met
simply by obedience, and a desire to communicate
in order to please God, not yourself. Again to
some the devil suggests thoughts of impurity, or
unbelief at the very moment they are about to
communicate—it may be even a doubt in the Real
Presence Itself; thus distracting the soul, so that it
loses all self-control ; or sometimes he disturbs the
senses and imagination in a like manner. Now, all
masters in the spiritual life without exception tell
us that these distractions must be treated with contempt, and that they are much rather a reason to
lead us to the Altar than to drive us thence. Their
object is manifest—to deter us from Communion,
and if we are so deterred, the devil succeeds in his
object. If we resist, we conquer. Some will say,
"But what if I receive unworthily?" Do not try to
decide for yourself; if your director is satisfied you
are safe;—but if you draw back from Communion
every time that the devil tries to persuade you
that you are not fit, you will end by never
communicating at all, and he will attain his
object, and deprive you of all your spiritual
strength. Holy Communion binds us to the
Cross of Christ, and the effect of receiving it
upon your soul will vary according to your special

condition and need. It may bring you sweetness, or it may be seemingly cold and painful, as you know your prayers are wont to be according to God's dealings within you. Nevertheless, "your life is hid with Christ in God." "Continue; . . . watch with thanksgiving."[1]

1 Col. iii. 2.

The Cross of Christ

" I DETERMINED," says St. Paul, " not to
know anything among you, save Jesus Christ
and Him Crucified."[1]   That is the substance of a
Christian's faith and practice.   In the Cross we
learn all the power of sin, the intensity of our
weakness, the far greater intensity of God's Mercy.
It is the all-prevailing witness of God's Love—the
most powerful attraction to man's heart. All graces
are to be found therein, and it is the perfection of
the interior life.   The Cross is the substance of our
faith, inasmuch as it sets before us the Only Son of
God, conceived by the Holy Ghost of the Virgin
Mary, and thus embodying the doctrines of the
Holy Trinity and of the Incarnation. It sets before
us the mystery of original sin and of redemption,
as of saving grace ; it is the fountain whence all
the Sacraments flow, the point to which all worship
tends.   The Cross is the substance of our practice,

1 1 Cor. ii. 2.

inasmuch as the whole lesson of the Gospel is to teach us to bear our Cross, to renounce self, and the lusts of the world, to give ourselves up to God. Every precept which our Dear Lord has given us, may be summed up in the doctrine of the Cross. It teaches us the power of sin, inasmuch as nothing less than the death of God made Man could crush that power, and atone for sin ;—the intensity of our weakness, for what remedy could we have brought had Christ not vouchsafed to be our Propitiation ? —the intensity of God's Mercy—for " if He spared not His Son, shall He not also freely give us all things ?" Can we meditate on these things and refuse the only return God asks of us—that we should love, serve, and obey Him ? Yet we count His yoke a burden, His commandments grievous, and Christians, with the Cross before their eyes, too often commit sins of which heathens might be ashamed ! Men even mock at the Cross of Christ. Yet surely one glance at the Crucifix should speak a whole volume to us of love, confidence, resigna- tion, patience, charity, and forgiveness to those who have wronged us, humility, lowliness. Can you look at your Crucifix and complain that your re- ligion costs too great a sacrifice ? that God exacts too much of you ? One glance there should surely

silence all murmurs at the trifles which perplex and
harass our daily life. What are they to the humiliation and Sufferings of our Incarnate Lord?

The Cross is the perfection of all interior life.
There we see Christ both Priest and Victim, voluntarily offering Himself to the glory and justice
of His Father, and though but few of us are called
to His Likeness, all who seek the interior life must
be fashioned according to it, and when the discip-
line seems more than they can bear, let them look
upon the Cross, and take fresh courage.

Be sure that there is no book like your Crucifix
—wherein not your eyes only read, but your heart.
Ask Jesus to be your teacher therein, to unfold its
manifold secrets, that you may not merely gaze
thereon, but live thereby. Seek the interior life
by total unreserved self-devotion to God's Will,—
accept every sacrifice He may require, ask Him to
take forcibly what you have not courage or strength
to give Him. "If I be lifted up from the earth, I
will draw all men unto me."[1] "He that taketh
not his cross, and followeth after Me, is not worthy
of Me."[2]

The Cross truly is the summary of Christ's
Gospel—the Christian's standard. But although

[1] John xii. 32.   [2] Matt. x. 38.

He saved us by His Cross, we are not exempted
from bearing ours; but rather all those are irre-
trievably pledged to it, who would follow their
Divine Master. Our Cross is sanctified by His,
without which the sharpest sufferings we can bear
would be of no avail before God to put away one
act of sin, or to open the Gates of Paradise for us.
All this we know well, but too often we fail to
reduce our knowledge to that practice which brings
the Cross home to us with its own special grace,
i.e., a daily dying to self. Yet Jesus Himself has
emphatically declared that this is the necessary
condition of enlisting under His banner. What
then is it to take up the Cross? and is it in truth
as heavy a burden as the natural man is ready to
believe? First of all, taking up the Cross involves
a diligent avoiding of sin, and of all occasions of
sin. This sounds only reasonable, but it is no easy
matter. Sin is often attractive and convenient; it
is sometimes attended with temporal advantages;
we are frequently, it may be daily, exposed to its
temptations, which are often urgent and delusive.
No Christian can withstand them without vigorous
and stedfast exertions. Next, taking up the Cross
consists in mortifying passions, restraining desires,
subjecting the flesh to the spirit, watching over the

senses, and all those feelings and imaginations
which influence the heart—for the heart is a source
whence evil springs—we tend of ourselves to sin,
and every earnest mind knows full well that without continued watchfulness we are sure to fall.

Again, taking up the Cross implies a weaning of
the heart and mind from things earthly, casual,
sensual, in order to fill them with that which is
heavenly, spiritual, eternal ; and this again requires
a perpetual struggle with our fallen nature, which
is ever drawing us downward. Watch yourself
honestly, and you will see how, without such a
struggle, your thoughts and wishes revert to earth,
and the comforts and conveniences of life. It is
no easy thing to keep the heart disentangled from
these aims and longings which inevitably lower the
spiritual tone. Further, the Cross requires us to
receive all that troubles us, whether from natural
causes, our own fault, or that of other men, as
coming from God's Hand. Such troubles are
ceaselessly recurring ; the more God loves us, the
more He lets us be tried by them, because they
detach us from the world, and draw us to Himself.
So with the mental trials which are closely inter-
woven in all our spiritual life, and which more
closely affect those who are seeking the interior

ways of holiness. These, above all, are linked to Christ's own Cross, and those who would follow His steps must share His humiliations, interior and exterior—a sharp Cross which pierces the very secrets of the soul; in comparison of which all the rest are light, which has no limit save in the total annihilation of self-love and self-seeking.

This latter Cross is laid but on a few souls; it is one, not of necessity but of love, and for that reason its weight is so heavy—love being tenfold as strong as mere duty. In some one or other of these shapes the Cross is laid on all Christians, good or bad, for these last are not exempt from God's providential Crosses, and their own passions involve them in many more. But now let us examine whether the Cross is really so heavy a burden as the natural heart of man is ready to believe it to be? One might well assert that there is no true happiness where the Cross is not, and that he who is lost has more to endure than he who is saved; that the wicked suffer hopelessly, miserably, and that even from this low ground the Cross is a blessing. But not to dwell on this general view, let us pass to details. If it is often hard work to avoid all occasions of sin, does conscience suffer nothing when we neglect such efforts, and do we not pay a heavy price for every indulgence in what we know to be wrong? Is there no gain in a peaceful heart which cleaves to God in temptation? Are not our passions so many hard tyrants, which give no rest to their slaves; and do they not cause many a weary heartache, even from a temporal point of view? Is he not to be pitied whose soul is subject to his body, dependent upon comforts and luxuries? Are not sorrows and disappointments easier to bear when offered up to God, than when we resist their pressure? and do not spiritual Crosses bring with them so exquisite a nearness to God, that the saints have cried out longingly, "More, ever more, Lord Jesus!"

God Only

THE whole spirit of the interior life is summed
up in the words " God Only." The first step
therein is devotion of self to Him—all progress in
it is detachment from whatever is not Him, and its
end is perfect union with Him. None save those
to whom this blessed union is given can conceive
its sweetness, but we can all study the trials whereby it is attained, the purity necessary to its attainment, and it is a point which every soul must learn
for itself. God Alone can lead us to this union, we
cannot win it for ourselves, the wisest director cannot win it for us. All man can do is to give himself unreservedly to God, and let Him work all His
good pleasure in the soul. In all things where his
co-operation is required, it must be diligently
rendered—not a word, a look, a desire however
innocent but must be sacrificed to God ; and no
thought of what will be said by others, what consequences may arise, no natural disinclinations, no
suggestions of the devil must be allowed to inter-

fere with this complete acquiescence in all God's
dealings. When God has taken sole possession of
the soul, faculties, memory, understanding, and will,
it must go on calmly, not seeking to penetrate His
purposes. God may seem to forsake the soul, all
refreshment and consolation may be taken away,
desolation and loneliness may be the very atmosphere it lives in, but the interior soul must go
on in stedfast patience, trusting in God, and
certain that He will "do all·things well." Such a
soul will find God's leading Hand in his spiritual
guide, who must be trusted and obeyed as for
God's Sake only. Should God even withdraw such
help from the soul, it is doubtless a grievous trial,
but if He Himself vouchsafes to be our guide, what
more need we ask? I would repeat again and
again, no plans or methods, no book, no director
can lead the soul to God Only. None, save He
Himself, can draw us, and unite us to Himself.
He knows the wants and capacities of each several
soul, let Him work as He will, while we follow His
guidance patiently and firmly.

If you ask what you must renounce? there is but
one answer, All save God. But inasmuch as none
of us can thoroughly fathom this renunciation, we
must leave it to God to teach us the lesson, and set

before us the sacrifices He requires of us. Do not
fear. Earthly imagination will paint such detachment in very alarming colours, human reason will
tell us that it is unattainable ; but turn to the Cross
in faith, meditate upon Christ's Passion, and you
will gain a truer notion of what self-renunciation
means. Ask Him to give you light, and to teach
you the meaning of those wondrous words, " It is
finished "—" Father, into Thy Hands I commend
My Spirit." Ask Him to make known to you what
it was He did when He gave us His Soul in expia-
tion of your sin. Before such truths imagination
and reason will melt away, and faith alone abide.
But do not be presumptuous. Remember Who it
was that said, " Father, if it be possible, let this
cup pass from Me." If for our sakes the Son of
God vouchsafed to endure such shrinking from the
sacrifice He had come on earth to make, how
greatly must we need His Grace to tread ever so far
off in His sacred steps ? Rather let us humble ourselves to the dust in consciousness of our own
weakness and helplessness, remembering the while
that God is All-Powerful, and that He can work
His own good pleasure in us, His poor, weak
children:—God Only. No more self, no more of
this world. GOD ONLY.

Continual Prayer

JESUS Christ said "that men ought always to pray, and not to faint;" and St. Paul bids us "pray without ceasing." What is meant thereby, and how can we fulfil the precept? Obviously vocal prayer is not intended: that must have definite limits, and so must the actual practice of mental prayer. Neither can the mind be continually occupied with direct thoughts of God and of spiritual matters. Human intelligence could not achieve an unbroken attention to God's Presence, even were such a mental process compatible with due attention to the duties of life. But then how are we to fulfil our Lord's injunction? By the heart's prayer, which consists in a constant habitual love of God, trusting Him, submitting in all things to His Will; and by giving a never-failing heed to His Voice, as heard within the conscience. This is how His Saints have prayed "without ceasing," and this it is which forms what we call the Interior life. God calls all men to this kind of prayer. Our Dear Lord did not say that His disciples only ought always to pray; and doubtless all who will really try to live such a life will find upholding grace. Try so to live in the light of God's Love that it becomes a second nature to you, tolerate nothing adverse to it, be continually striving to please Him in all things, take all He sends patiently; resolve firmly never to commit the smallest deliberate fault, and if unhappily you are overtaken by any sin, humble yourself and rise up speedily. Thus you will indeed "pray without ceasing." Such prayer will go on amid all your occupations and pursuits, even amid your innocent amusements. It is neither impossible, or even difficult. You will not always be thinking formally of God, but all your thoughts will be ruled by Him; His Presence will check useless or evil thoughts; you will not make perpetual acts of Love or faith, but your heart will be perpetually fixed on Him, ready to do His Holy Will.

It is a great mistake to fancy that all real prayer must be direct, formal, conscious. Many people suppose that they are not really praying unless their intellect or feelings are aroused, and thus they grow discouraged. But God sees "the preparation of the heart;"—He needs neither words or thoughts of ours to set the true disposition of our heart before Him—the prayer of will, as yet undeveloped into form, scarcely perceived by us, is as plain to Him as our most overt act. St. Anthony said that the best prayers were those in which we are unconscious that we pray: at all events self-love can find no food therein..

But though such continual prayer is not difficult, it is rare, because so few have courage to persevere. Nor can it be attained without giving yourself wholly to God,—and few souls give themselves unreservedly to Him, there are so many secret hindrances set in the way by self-love. But once give yourself freely to Him, and He will forthwith give you Himself, He will dwell in your heart, and kindle that spirit of prayer which will cause you to be calm and re-collected amid all your daily duties. At first, you will be conscious of this recollection, and rejoice in it, but after a time it becomes purely spiritual, and you cannot renew the consciousness of its existence without fostering self-love. But do not suppose that you are ceasing to pray always because you cannot feel it; above all, do not give up any of your habitual devotions from an idea that you are not really praying. It is simply a temptation to seek consolation in the creature rather than in God.

If you would persevere in this continual prayer, try to realise that the less conscious it is, the more acceptable to God. Avoid as far as possible all self-inspection which tends to feed self-complacency. Resist the suggestion that your prayers and communions are unprofitable, because you have no conscious sweetness in them ;—such thoughts come from the devil. Believe that God knows what He is doing, and trust yourself to Him. Be stedfast in shunning creature consolations, give no way to dissipating thoughts, and if you are called to give up even the most innocent pleasures of life, do so willingly. By degrees you will feel that God reigns supreme in you, He will train you in the love of silence and solitude, He will wean you from the world and its interests, purify your senses, and fill you with His sanctifying grace. As you cease to be conscious of praying always, you will be more detached even from spiritual consolations, you will die more to all love of self, you will grow in simplicity and in nearness to God. Then He will train you to offer yourself by whatever interior or exterior crosses He requires—even temptation, desolation and seeming loss of Himself, if such be His Holy Will. And

through this mystical death, He will bring you forth
to a joyful spiritual resurrection, which even in this
life has a share of that which is to come hereafter
for all His faithful followers.   " If we be dead with
Him, we shall also live with Him : if we suffer, we
shall also reign with Him."[1]

[1] 1 Tim. ii. 12.

Confidence in God

THERE is no point in the spiritual life so essential as this; without it, the soul is powerless, with it, we can do all things. Confidence in God is beset by two enemies, both of which must be guarded against; on the one hand presumption, cowardice on the other. Presumption raises a false conception of the Mercy of God, and leads to its abuse, or to slackness in our efforts to attain perfection. It is wont to say that God will not heed little things, or exact an over-strict account. Cowardice is so beset with the terror of God's judgments, that it loses sight of His Mercy, and often verges on despair. Both extremes arise from self-love and distorted views : the true course is to trust wholly in God, neither presuming or desponding, but this true course can only be attained by those who give themselves sincerely to God. As a general rule, men are most liable to err on the side of presumption, and women on that of fearfulness and mistrust.

I

Confidence in God is based on a knowledge of Him and of ourselves. The first teaches us His Infinite Goodness, His Love for His children, and the certainty that He wills nothing but their good. It reminds us of the work of Redemption He has wrought for us, of His ever-present Grace, His readiness to receive and forgive the penitent sinner, His longing desire to recall the wandering sheep. Who can retrace his own past life and not see the abundant signs of God's Mercy which have visited him? the occasions of sin averted or overruled, His long-suffering when we fell, His manifold gifts and graces whereby we have been led and upheld, through which alone we have been preserved hitherto? Recall all the individual graces which you have received, and be sure that those of which you are unconscious are tenfold in number. On the other hand, the more we know of ourselves, the more cause we shall find to put all our trust in God. Of myself I can do absolutely nothing as regards my supernatural life; I am not merely weak, I am powerless. I can misuse my liberty to lose my soul, but I cannot save it through my own free-will; I need the stay of God's never-failing Grace, and that I know will be granted to trustful prayer. When I fall I cannot arise, save by the help of

God's Hand, but I know that it will be stretched forth the moment that I claim its help. I cannot count on the strength of my own intentions, or resolutions, or promises ; still less can I dare alone to face the dangers and temptations which beset a Christian's life. In short, the whole work of my salvation, from first to last, depends upon God. He can prosper it, and in spite of all my weakness and perversity, He will bring it to a safe end, if I do but cleave stedfastly to Him. The more humble a man is, the stronger his confidence in God will be, and confidence grounded on humility will never be presumptuous. But neither will that be a cowardly confidence which is built on a certainty of His Infinite Goodness and Love. Who can be afraid while stayed upon his God. "Cast yourself freely into His Arms," says St. Augustine, "and never fear that He will let you fall." What foe can touch us, what temptation can soil us within those Everlasting Arms ?

You say that God's Justice is very terrible. Unquestionably ; but to whom is it terrible ? Not to His children who love and serve Him, who have given themselves to Him body and soul ? He loves them more than they love Him. He knows their every fault, but He knows how much is mere

human frailty and imperfection ; it needs but one
sorrowful loving glance to win His forgiveness, and
if He chastens them, it is with a tender Hand and
for their true blessing.   Is His justice terrible to the
true penitent ?   Surely not.   God's Mercy is even
more overflowing to such than to the "just who
need no repentance."   God's Justice is in truth
terrible to none save those who, out of presumption
or despair, fail to seek His Mercy ; to those who
will not forsake their sins, or to those who deal in
crooked ways, and would fain deceive God Himself
were it possible.   Such as these neither have or
can have any true confidence in God ; they have
no claim to it until they heartily grieve because
they have displeased Him, and seek to turn to
Him.   He would have men fear His Justice, that
they may flee from sin, through repentance, and
that they may never delude themselves by thinking
their repentance sufficient.   But, at the same time,
He would have us put entire trust in Him and His
Mercy, and turn to Him rather from love than
fear, without idle terrors which hinder true penitence, and are an insult to His Goodness.

Shrinking souls are apt to raise difficulties.   How
far is this trust to go ? they ask.   As far as the
limits of His Power and Goodness, of our weakness

and misery, can reach. We must go boldly on, unscared by danger or difficulty. As regards yourself you may well say, "I can do nothing," but look to God as your Guide and Strength, and you may dare to say, "I can do all things." Do you fear the world? "Be not afraid, I have overcome the world;" and as our Dear Lord overcame it in His Own Blessed Person, so He will overcome it in yours. The world is not a greater difficulty to us than it was to the saints who have trodden its wilderness before us; and they had no more strength of themselves than we have : their strength was all of God, and by His Grace we may be strong as they. Do you fear the snares of the devil? He becomes powerless in the presence of humble confidence in God. If you do not presume upon your own strength, but look solely to God, all the powers of hell cannot prevail against you.

Do you feel painfully that self-love hinders everything, and is for ever thwarting your best efforts? Be watchful against its attempts—mistrust your own will and judgment ; and as you grow daily in the Love of God, you will daily weaken the bonds of self-love. Set aside all your own interests for those of God, and leave Him to provide for you. Do not strive to make His Will fit into yours, but

give up your own will to Him for time and for
eternity. By degrees His Love will banish self.
Do you dread the trials and humiliations involved
in thus putting the natural man to death?   In
truth it is a harder struggle than we can well
imagine, but the more heartily you gird youself to
the attempt, the more God will uphold you in it.
Your courage and your strength will grow in por-
portion as you lose sight of self, and with His Aid
you will triumph over all, the world, the devil, self-
love.   " Perfect love casteth out all fear," save only
the fear of displeasing God, or of refusing aught
He asks.

How we must Love God

STRANGE that it should be needful to urge man to love God, his Author and his End, the Source of every blessing he enjoys! One would have thought that self-interest alone was enough to kindle such love. "Thou biddest me love Thee, O my God," exclaims St. Augustine, "as though the greatest misfortune that can reach me were not to fail in loving Thee!" Nevertheless it is the first and chiefest precept He has given us, "Thou shalt love the Lord thy God with all thy heart, and all thy soul, and all thy strength, and all thy mind."

"Thou shalt love," with a love as far beyond other love as God is above all that can call it forth—not by fits and snatches, or uncertainly, but stedfastly from the first dawning of reason till your last breath. It must be your abiding moral condition.

"Thou shalt love the Lord thy God"—He who is Infinite, Perfect, Holy—the Source of all holiness. You are bound to Him by every possible tie and gift in the past and present, by every hope of the future. You are to love Him with all your mind, the faculties of which were given you that you might know Him. He must be ever in your thoughts, banishing whatever might be displeasing or dero-gatory to Him; and this includes a right use of your understanding as concerns His service, and the duties of your position, in short, of all that forms a stedfast Christian life.

You must "love Him with all your heart," ever ready to give up everything, to bear everything rather than sin against His Love. Such love will raise you above all mere sensuality, human respect, worldly profit or loss. "He who will lose his life shall find it."

You must "love Him with all your strength ;"— without measure or limit, ever seeking to grow in that love, through prayer, Sacraments, good works, sufferings, or whatsoever may be the course appoint-ed for you. Now many well meaning persons are greatly troubled to know whether they really love God thus heartily? Such persons may take com-fort from the thought that this very anxiety is a sure proof that they do love Him, though as such trouble and anxiety may become excessive through self-love, it is well to submit the question to a wise

confessor, and then to abstain from perpetually re-
opening it.

Again we must not measure the reality of love by
feelings, but by results.   Feelings are very delusive.
They often depend on mere natural temperament,
and the devil wrests them to our hurt.   A glowing
imagination is apt to seek itself rather than God.
But if you are earnest in striving to serve and endure for God's Sake, if you persevere amid temptation, dryness, weariness and desolation, you may
rest assured that your love is real.   As men advance
in the interior life, they learn to indulge less and
less in self-dissection, even as regards their love of
God;—they are content to give themselves up to
Him in this matter as in all else—to love Him
without any conscious dwelling upon their love ;
and this is the higher and purer form of love.   It is
free from all self-complacency, absorbed in God
Himself.   Its "life is hid with Christ in God," and
any self-inspection would be a risk.

As a rule it is not well to make many conscious
efforts or much self-examination, with a view to
increasing or preserving this love.   Dwelling on the
Love of God for us, a pure intention, constant self-
renunciation, and faithfulness to the leadings of
grace, are better means for its growth in the heart.

All love comes from God ;—He implants it there,
He Alone nourishes it, He Alone knows what it
should be.   Let us leave it to Him, and " He Who
has begun the good work" will perfect it.   Christ
said, " I am come to send fire on the earth, and
what will I, if it be already kindled ?"   Let us offer
our hearts to the blaze of that gracious fire—once
kindled it will never die out of itself, but will rather
burn up all that is earthly and impure within us,
till having consumed self, it will absorb us into its
own heat.

Rest in God

" Come to Me. all ye that labour and are heavy laden, and I will give you rest."—MATT. xi. 28

WHO but would test this gracious promise? Who is free from the heavy load of pain, either bodily, mental, or spiritual? Yet how many spend half their lives in vainly seeking rest? If ever there was a question which it concerns us all to answer, it is this, Where is Rest to be found?

The larger part of mankind seek it in wealth, in honours, in worldly ease; but they do not find it. Covetousness, greed, envy, fraud, conspire to spoil all thought of rest in the good things of this world. Others seek rest in themselves, but what can be expected from our weak, changeable natures? Society, literature, science, may occupy, but they cannot satisfy or rest the heart. There is no rest for the heart of man save in God, Who made him for Himself.[1] But how shall we rest in God? By

[1] "Fecisti nos propter Te, et inquietum est cor nostrum, donec perveniat ad Te."—August. Conf. i. 1.

giving ourselves wholly to Him. If you give yourself by halves, you cannot find full rest—there will
ever be a lurking disquiet in that half which is
withheld; and for this reason it is that so few
Christians attain to a full, stedfast, unchanging
peace—they do not seek rest in God only, or give
themselves up to Him without reserve. True rest
is as unchanging as God Himself—like Him it rises
above all earthly things: it is secret, abundant,
without a regret or a wish. It stills all passion,
restrains the imagination, steadies the mind, con-
trols all wavering : it endures alike in the "time of
tribulation and the time of wealth ;" in temptation
and trial, as when the world shines brightly on us.
Martyrs, confessors, and saints have tasted this
rest, and "counted themselves happy in that they
endured." A countless host of God's faithful
servants have drunk deeply of it amid the daily
burden of a weary life—dull, commonplace, painful,
or desolate. All that God has been to them He
is ready to be to you; He only asks that you should
seek no other rest save in Him.

It is a rest which has never failed those who
honestly sought it. The heart once fairly given to
God, with a clear conscience, a fitting rule of life,
and a stedfast purpose of obedience, you will find

a wonderful sense of rest coming over you. What
once fretted you, ceases to do so ; former unworthy
exciting pleasures cease to attract you. No miser
ever so feared to lose his treasure, as the faithful
soul fears to lose this rest when once tasted. Such
words may seem exaggeration to those who have
not tried it ; but the Saints will tell you otherwise.
St. Paul will tell you of a "peace which passeth
understanding ;" Jesus Christ tells you of His
Peace, which the world can neither give or take
away, because it is God's Gift only. Such peace
may undergo many an assault, but it will but be
confirmed thereby, and rise above all that would
trouble it. He who has tasted it would not give it
in exchange for all this life can give ; and death is
to him a passage from this rest to that of Eternity.

The Soul's Life

"Seek ye after God, and your soul shall live."—Psa. lxix. 33

HEREIN lies the root of our duty, and of all happiness. Happiness is the soul's life; without happiness, or the hope thereof, life seems not worth having. What is this happiness, and how is it to be found? Holy Scripture tells us, in God Only; and "our life is hid with Christ in God." Just as the body becomes a prey to corruption, when its union with the soul is dissolved, so the soul depends for life upon its union with God; yet not after a wholly self-same manner. The body contains an inherent principle of corruption, whereas the soul has an inherent principle of life— *i.e.* its faculty of knowledge and love. But were these to be expended on itself alone, the soul's life must inevitably deteriorate, and, as a natural consequence, it is ever reaching forth towards objects more satisfying wherein to rest. Such rest is not to be found in the things of sense; "the Spirit giveth life," and it alone; and until the soul drinks, and drinks deeply of the Spirit of God, it will not find its true life. He kindles the burning thirst which leads us to the fountain of living water, and He has promised to satisfy it abundantly; but He will have us ask before He gives, and to that end He has taught us to use the blessed grace of prayer. The soul cannot die, in the sense of ceasing to exist, but its death consists in ceasing to know or love God; and weary indeed is that man's life who has turned away from these saving truths—to him all is restlessness and anxiety, fretting desires, unful-filled hopes—no peace, no light, no satisfaction. But he who has found his soul's life in God is happy —not in truth with perfect happiness; that is not granted to men in this world, but a foretaste thereof —he has a secret joy which is beyond the reach of temptation, unrest and sorrow; a quiet confidence and stedfastness which abide even while the waves and storms of life sweep over him. God has promised, not that he shall be free from crosses, rather they form the ladder by which the soul mounts upwards, but that He will abide with His faithful servant through them all, and be his Rock, his Castle, his strong Foundation. In this world he may suffer loss—" the Lord killeth and maketh alive : He bringeth down to the grave, and bringeth up ; the Lord maketh poor, and maketh rich, He bringeth low and lifteth up;"[1] but while "death worketh in us," in our senses and passions, our human spirit and will, it is "that the life of Jesus might be made manifest in us ;" the life of love, of glory, of perfect happiness for the soul.

1 1 Sam. ii. 6, 7.

The Soul's Peace

" Great is the peace that they have who love Thy law."—Ps. cxix. 165

THIS peace will not be won by mere literal obedience; God's law must be loved as well as obeyed; there must be the filial spirit as well as the legal duty rendered. Those who obey God's law only because they fear His judgments, cannot look for the overflowing peace and joy which are the reward of a loving service; a service which confesses heartily that His "yoke is easy, His burden light," and which aims at promoting His Glory rather than any reward. Not that such a spirit in any way ignores the fear of hell or the hope of Heaven, but it is raised to something beyond them both. When the soul has sincerely given itself up to God, He fills it with His own peace, a peace which makes all earthly things indifferent—as before His Presence, absorbing the heart. It is our strength, our comfort, our guide;—the deeper and more confirmed it becomes, the greater our spiritual per-

K

fection; so that in truth to obtain and preserve this peace is the real secret of the interior life.   There are a few simple rules which may help the soul in this blessed work.   And, first, enjoy such peace as you do the gift of health, without constantly examining into it.   If you were to be always feeling your pulse to see whether you were well or ill, you would probably end by making yourself ill ; and it is equally unwise to be for ever gauging the soul's peace.   It is easy to confuse real peace with what is a mere matter of feeling.   In the earlier stages peace brings great conscious sweetness, but this may pass away without any real loss ; just as after a severe illness, we are alive to each degree of returning strength, and when fully restored to health, we do not notice what is habitual to us.   Next try to act with simplicity, not thinking overmuch about your actions, either present or past ;—all anxious self-searching is hurtful to peace.   If your conscience does not reproach you, it is needless to cross question it; it is enough that you give diligent heed when its whispers are heard, and a perpetual self-torture and questioning as to whether your intentions are right or wrong tends to nothing save perplexity and rest-lessness.   Be sure that vague general fears are rather the work of your imagination than of God or your conscience. Fears that you have not said all you ought in confession, that you did not explain yourself properly, that your contrition was imperfect, that you did not receive Holy Communion with fitting dispositions, and the like vague fretting apprehensions are not of God. When He stirs the soul to fear it has sinned, it is always with a clear definite reproach;—you must learn to despise and set aside those self-dissections. Again, bear in mind that God never casts the soul into trouble and anxiety when it is truly seeking Him. He warns, He rebukes, but He never troubles you;—He enables you to see your fault, to repent and make amends, but it is all done calmly—restlessness and anxiety are the devil's work, and to be withstood. Moreover, it is a most important point never to change your spiritual course, because of any such troubles : prayer, Communions, all your devotional exercises must be persevered in, and you will ere long conquer Satan and regain peace. Obedience to your director is another great help in the attainment of peace, setting aside as that does the delusions of self-love. Above all, beware of letting go the spirit of peace because of your faults. Humble yourself before God because of them, repent, make such reparation for them as you are able, and then do not dwell upon them any more. It is often mere pride which frets at finding itself beset by the same often renewed faults, and at its lack of spiritual progress. Do not deceive yourself into the belief that such disquiet is humility. A really humble soul accepts its faults with patience, and goes afresh on in confidence and hope.

The Spirit of Faith

"THE just shall live by faith." St. Paul is not speaking here of our dogmatic faith, but of that which is purely personal, and which specially concerns God's Providence over the souls He leads. Such souls He inspires with perfect trust in His Word and promise, and then He tries the strength of that trust, by various searching tests, through which it is their part to remain stedfast, undoubting, "hoping against hope," as St. Paul says. Holy Scripture is full of examples of such faith. "I know in Whom I have believed."

Bodily sufferings, spiritual trials, desolation, humiliation, the Cross in infinite variety is laid upon God's chosen servants, but the Spirit of faith upholds them; they never seek to take back the gift they have given Him—even their whole heart; or desire to throw aside His guiding Hand, however heavily it may sometimes press. Their soul cries out with Job, "Though He slay me yet will I trust in Him," and such a spirit at once promotes God's glory and their own hidden life. Satan fears such a spirit of faith before all things, knowing that where it is found he can never prevail; and he spares no pains to undermine it by every conceivable assault of unbelief, intellectual pride, or ignorance; by taunting those who act under its influence with hypocrisy, folly, extravagance, what not! Be it ours to combat him by ever renewed faith, by renewing the very acts from which he would turn us. Our God is the Mighty, the True, the Faithful God; Heaven and earth will pass away, but His Word will never pass away; they will pass away before He will fail those who trust in Him. He does but try and test our love, and what is that love worth which cannot bear to be tested? His trials may be exceeding great, inasmuch as He is God, and there is no limit to the love He requires of us. Blessed is that soul which He tries thus, even though the trial seem well nigh overwhelming: "Love is strong as death; jealousy is cruel as the grave;—the coals thereof are coals of fire, which hath a most vehement flame. Many waters cannot quench love, neither can the floods drown it." (Cant. viii. 6, 7.)

Love for our Neighbour

"A new commandment I give unto you, that ye love one another, as I have loved you."—JOHN xiii. 34

MUTUAL love had been a natural law since the world began, why then did our Lord call it a new commandment? Because He gave an altogether new aspect to the ancient law when He bade men take His Example as the measure of their love—as the proof that they were His true followers, and His Love was boundless, even to the death of the Cross. Through that great Love, He has bound all men together as members of a vast supernatural family, of which God is the Father, Jesus Christ Himself the Brother; all have a claim to the same eternal heritage, all share the same grace, the same Sacraments, all are fed with the same Living Bread, all are One in Christ. How then shall we not love one another? And if we do indeed take His Example as our standard of love, we shall find that it binds us to give freely of our

best, not in temporal things only, but in spiritual;
to be liberal in prayer and intercession, ever to remember how much good or harm our example does
among our brethren, always to be ready to forgive
and forbear. If Christians really followed out their
Saviour's precept, we should see no quarrels, no
scandal given or taken, no antipathies, no harsh
judgments, no unkind acts or words. Yet, practically, we often shew as little of this true spirit of
charity as the heathen themselves. Self-love is the
source of all evil, and not less destructive of true
love of man, than of God. It concentrates men
within themselves and their own interests, so that
they look upon their neighbour's interests, temporal
and spiritual, as a thing apart, until estrangement,
envy and jealousy overpower better influences, and
it may be even that a brother's spiritual progress is
looked upon grudgingly as though it were an injury
to our credit and appearance of holiness. All extreme sensitiveness, fastidiousness, suspicion, readiness to take offence, and tenacity of what we think
our due, come from this self-love, as does the unworthy secret gratification we sometimes feel when
another is humbled or mortified; the cold indifference, the harshness of our criticism, the unfairness
and hastiness of our judgments, our bitterness

towards those we dislike, and many other faults
which must more or less rise up before most men's
conscience, when they question it sincerely as to
how far they do indeed love their neighbours as
Christ has loved them ?

Perhaps no one can attain to full perfection in
this law of love, who is not more or less leading an
interior life; and that because it involves a constant
mortification of a man's own mind and will, a constant subjection thereof to the mind of Christ. The
occasions of sinning against perfect charity are perpetually arising in one shape or other, and if you
are not watchful, self-love will establish an ever-
increasing hold upon your heart, imperceptibly
misleading your judgment, and warping your
affections. Many very excellent people betray a
great deal of harshness and want of charity in
judging their neighbours, and you may be sure that
the source is self-love and a lack of interior life;
these imperfections are of such a subtle nature that
they cannot be seen save by the help of a supernatural light ; very trifles in appearance often need
no small effort if we would deal rightly with them,
and great self-renunciation is sometimes involved in
seemingly trivial matters. It may sound strange,
but I believe truly that it is harder to love our

neighbour perfectly than to love God, though of
course really the two things are inseparable. But
the greater part of the faults committed by religious
minded people concern their neighbours in some
shape or other, and there are many more which
they neither see or suspect, and of which they would
be hard to convince. Those, however, who are
sincerely seeking to live an interior life, and to be
led wholly by God's Grace, will escape many of
these delusions of self-love. They are continually
listening to God's Voice within their heart, and
striving by His guidance to give a constant preference to what promotes others' welfare rather than
to their own. That Voice will not fail to make
itself heard when there is any danger of a breach
of the law of perfect love; no unkind word, not
even an uncharitable smile or gesture, escapes God's
Eye, and He will shew His servants wherein they
have sinned; He will check their unspoken judgments, suspicions and imputations; He will root out
all dislikes and aversions, all readiness to take
offence, all resentments, all bitterness from the heart
which is given up to His guidance. He will infuse
His own tender Love for man into His servant's
mind, and teach him to "love his brother as Christ
has loved him." But this can only be looked for

by those who live in a constant spirit of prayer, ever watchful for the Holy Spirit's whispers within, ever diligent in obeying His leadings. And this is the true interior life.

The World

EVERY one who seeks to give himself to God,
and to attain everlasting life, is deeply concerned in the questions, What is the world? and
How far does it concern a Christian? Holy Scripture answers the first query. It is the "enemy of
Christ." The world consists of those men who
look for happiness in the things of sense, and dread
poverty, suffering, humiliation, as the real evils of
life, which are to be averted at any cost, while they
seek riches, honours, and pleasures with correspond-
ing energy; unscrupulous as to how such things are
attained, regardless of other men's interests where
these are concerned, despising those who do not
possess them. Prosperity is substantially the world's
code, its ruling spirit, its test of merit. But this
spirit is altogether contrary to that of Christ. He
told His disciples that it must be so. "If the
world hate you, ye know that it hated me before it
hated you; if ye were of the world, the world

would love his own; but because ye are not of the world, but I have chosen you out of the world, therefore the world hateth you." The world "could not receive the Spirit of truth," and those to whom He came were not to be "of the world." In the earliest days of the Church, it was easy to distinguish between those who were called out of the world by Christ. Idolatry and persecution were tests which made the line plain, but since Christianity has spread through civilised nations, a world has arisen amid Christians which, in spite of its nominal profession of a higher law, yet contrives to carry on most of the vices of idolatry, and to teach a code in all things the very opposite to the Gospel of Christ.

That nominal profession of Christianity, however, makes it hard to discern the snare—the world disguises its counsel skilfully, propagates its doctrine insidiously, and makes a great pretence of reconciling its laws with those of Christ, chiefly, it must be owned, by softening down the holy severity of His precepts. Nothing is so dangerous as the subtle spirit which steals upon men unawares, affecting to find an agreement between Christian strictness and the world's opinions, whether in general morals or daily practice. Such treacherous delusions are apt to invade even spiritually-minded men, and the

evil is harder to deal with than more open acts of
worldliness and wrong, which are more apparent
and unquestionable. But in truth there is but one
course to be taken by those who, while yet in the
world, would be " kept from the evil ;" it is that of
which St. Paul says, "the world is crucified unto
me, and I unto the world."[1] Crucifixion was the portion of slaves when the Apostle wrote these words,
and assuredly he meant to imply that the world
was an object of contempt, of loathing,—an accursed
thing, with which he would have no dealings, no
intercourse. The world had insulted, outraged,
crucified Jesus Christ,—it renews its insults daily
yet—how can the disciples do otherwise than hate
and renounce their Master's enemy ? The first act
of a Christian's life is a solemn renunciation of the
world in Holy Baptism, it is the essential condition
on which we are admitted into Christ's Church.
Do you often call this promise to mind, and the
obligations it involves ? There is no middle course ;
the world has its law, its doctrine, its course,—
Christ's law and doctrine and way are the very
opposite ; they are irreconcileable enemies. You
cannot halt between the two opinions, or remain
neutral. If you follow Christ and His Cross, the

[1] Gal. vi. 14.

world will disown you—if you follow the world, its pomps and vanities, Christ will reject you. Can you hesitate? But once take your place beneath the standard of the Cross, and count upon the world as your relentless enemy for ever.

Nor is it enough that "the world is crucified to me." We must be "crucified to the world;" that is, we must expect the hatred and insults, the contempts and assaults of the world. "If they have persecuted Me, they will persecute you also," Christ said to His disciples. The world would not be the world, or Christ's servants would not be truly His, were it otherwise. At times we are apt to long for some certainty as to our spiritual condition, whether we are indeed acceptable before God, whether Christ owns us as His? There is no better way of solving the question than by reflecting whether the world accepts and esteems us, seeks us out, speaks well of us? If so, we are none of Christ's! But if the world criticises, blames, despises, casts us out, let us be of good cheer, for then in truth we may hope that we are indeed numbered among the servants of Christ.

Do not shrink from examining closely as in God's Presence, how you stand with respect to the world, and the world to you. Search into your inner heart, weigh its motives. You will find abundant cause for dismay and humiliation ; you will find that the world has left its furrows in your mind, that too often your opinions are based upon the world's maxims; you will find that you look more than you fancied for its esteem, that you shrink from its contempt; that you cling to worldly connections, habits of life, forms and practices, solely out of human respect; and that thanks to such bondage you are often constrained and unreal. You will scarcely fail to find that as yet you have not sufficiently taken Christ's part against the world. But do not be discouraged. It is not the work of a day, you cannot put the world aside, and be content to be put aside by it all at once. Be watchful in little things, such as daily offer themselves. God will provide you with many opportunities, and trifling successes will train you for greater victories. Ever remember our Dear Lord's words, "Be of good cheer, I have overcome the world." He will enable you to overcome it—He will root out the world's spirit from your heart, and fill you wholly with His own.

"All that is not God is unworthy of man" may be taken as our standard; all else is unworthy to engross the mind and heart, or to be their chief aim and object. Remember that eternal life is your destiny, and that this earthly life is merely a preparation for it—think how insufficient the things of the world are to satisfy the cravings of your soul. Even in the happiest earthly moments we ever know here, the chief zest generally lies in some hope, some imagination of a future joy, rather than in actual reality; and considering all this, you will scarce deny that God Alone is capable of filling and satisfying the hearts He has made for Himself. But having granted the theory, you must reduce it to practice, and frame your life upon it. Thus you will abstain from immoderate cleaving to the things which are passing away; God gives you them to use as you travel through your time of probation, but He would not have you lean upon them, or seek all your rest therein; if you should do so, He will assuredly turn them into bitterness, and that for your own gain. You will also weigh in a just balance all the things after which the world runs most eagerly—the advantages of rank, honour, man's esteem. Are they worth so much as you may have been tempted to think? or is there good reason why you should pride yourself on their possession? Again, as to physical and intellectual advantages; are you more precious in God's Sight

L

because of them ? and if not, ought you to hold yourself as better than others who have them not ? Is
there any reason to take credit to yourself for personal beauty, or mental capacity ? Still less can
wealth, position, and their attendant circumstances,
be subjects of pride to a Christian, while health and
life itself are only precious in so far as they are
used to God's Glory. So the praise of man cannot
influence your future happiness, save in so far as it
may hinder you by exciting vanity and self-satisfaction. What then are all these things which we
so eagerly seek after worth ? If God only is worthy
of our love, that which He loves can alone be worth
our search ; and we know from our Saviour's own
lips, that "that which is highly esteemed among
men is abomination in the Sight of God."[1] He
measures all things by the standard of Eternity ;
men by that of the world and its passing gains.
He esteems the Cross, trial, suffering, humiliation,
all that detaches us from this life, and raises us to
Himself; men cleave to all that makes life smooth
and pleasant, while it veils the heavenly horizon.
Which is the safest course, which the path of true
happiness ?

If, then, you would follow the Saints who have

[1] Luke xvi. 15.

entered upon their blessed rest in Paradise, you must keep ever before your mind the maxim that whatever is not of God, whatever is not infinite, eternal, enduring, is unworthy of your love; that you are made for Him Only, and that nothing has any real value which does not draw you closer to Him, and strengthen your hope of your heavenly heritage. Your true guide through the perplexities around is Christ's Gospel, His doctrine, His example. He became Incarnate to teach us what the true dignity and worth of manhood is, and it is through Holy Scripture alone that man appears great—by reason of his approach to God; all human philosophy sets forward nought save the littleness of human nature, because God is not the Beginning, Centre, the End thereof.

Learn to tread under pride and vanity, self-conceit and earthliness, and you will attain to a dignity of which you little thought to be capable. " It doth not yet appear what we shall be, but we know that when He shall appear, we shall be like Him, for we shall see Him as He is."[1]

[1] 1 John iii. 2.

The Human Heart

" The heart is deceitful above all things, and desperately wicked, who can know it?"—JER. xvii. 9

BY "the heart" we must understand that hidden depth of evil, perversity and self-love, which is in us all, and which affects even our best actions more or less; for who that knows himself ever so little but is conscious how self-love tarnishes and hinders almost all he does? This is a consequence of original sin, which diverted what would have been our natural leaning to God, and turned the stream of our affections upon self. Deal honestly with yourself, and you will see that in fact we measure everything by the standard of self, by our own interests and opinions; whereas rightly we ought to refer all to God, His Spirit and Will. It is this disturbance of the right order of things which is at the root of all sin and destruction. Even in little children we see the daily growth of

this unholy self which is apt to make good its hold
in the heart before reason or religion have asserted
their claim. And the worst of it is that it is of the
very essence of this evil to blind us to ourselves ;—
we see the faults of others plainly enough, but not
our own ;—we are vexed with those who point them
out to us, we refuse to acknowledge them, and too
often when roused to consciousness of what is wrong
in us, we are rather irritated at what is humiliating
to our pride, then humbled by realising the truth.
Our great object is to disguise our own heart both
as regards ourselves and others. With the last we
do not always succeed, they are quicker to perceive
our faults ; but unhappily we are only too successful in evading that self-knowledge which is so
specially necessary to a Christian, yet so rare, so
seldom honestly sought. Men live and die without
having really tried to fathom their own hearts—
having rather tried all along to deceive themselves
to the utmost. But then what must it not be to
appear before an All-seeing God, Who is Truth itself, and in the blaze of His searching Light to see
all our own sinfulness, without veil or shadow? And
moreover, then it will be too late!

Surely it is best to strive now to measure one's self
by God's standard, fairly accepting both the exceed-

ing necessity of a real knowledge of self, and its great
difficulty. From childhood we have been heap-
ing up fresh hindrances in the way, but He Who
"knoweth the secrets of the heart," Who "numbers
our steps, and watches over our sin"[1] will give us
light if we ask it sincerely—light whereby to search
out our hidden motives, our inclinations and lean-
ings, the most subtle delusions of our heart. Above
all, we must be inexorably strict in acknowledging
the faults we discover, and abstain from all attempts
to justify ourselves to ourselves or to others. God
will not fail to shed His Light on the heart which
thus simply and sincerely confesses its blindness,
and he who rightly uses this first penetrating ray,
will advance daily in self-knowledge, he will learn
to disentangle the seeming confusion of self-deceit,
its wiles will melt before his stern resolution, and
with God's Help he will effectually rid himself of
his insidious foe.

It is well to bear in mind that God in His Wisdom
only gives the grace of self-knowledge gradually ;—
if He were to shew us our true selves suddenly,
we should despair, and lose all courage. But as we
perceive and conquer the more glaring faults, His
gracious Light shews us our subtler, more hidden

[1] Job xiv. 16.

imperfections; and this spiritual process lasts all through life. Happy he who, when the hour of death comes, has attained to a full knowledge of his soul's sickness, and a perfect measure of healing. Such grace appertains chiefly to those who are unsparing of self and faithful in rendering a strict account to God. The main thing is to go on in a straightforward path, guided by God's own Light, assured that he who swerves is lost; to mistrust one's own opinion, judgment and inclination, leaning solely on the Holy Spirit's guidance, deferring to Him in all things. But this is no easy matter, and it is a very death to self, as well as a rising again to perfection. It is a sure way to avoid mistakes: our own judgment is more often wrong than right, we err as to what true holiness is, and how to attain it; —we misjudge our own actions and motives, still more those of others;—we approve or condemn hastily and without due cause, and thereby we go perversely astray. All our faults arise from trusting in self rather than in God;—we are too heedless, too confident, not sufficiently humble;—we unconsciously let our own judgment usurp God's authority within us;—we imagine that we are following His Guidance while in truth we are rushing headlong after our own wild vagaries;—we shut our ears to wise counsel and restraint, and pass unheeding on our way. It may sound harsh, but it is a truth that people who have the best and most honest intentions are continually falling into very grievous faults, entirely from the lack of an interior spirit which would guard them against the attacks of self-love. There is but one safe course,—mistrust of self, taking God as your guide—renouncing your own way and will. However much progress you may have made, yield the reins to self, and you will fall back at once. The further you advance, the more you need Divine Light; and the greatest Saint who ever trod the earth would have perilled his salvation had he for a moment believed that he could go onwards without that Light. Rest assured then, that as your heart is such an unfathomable mystery, as self-love is so quick to seduce and blind you, as pride is ever striving to raise a barrier betwixt you and Heaven, your only safety is in holding fast to God, renewing acts of self-mistrust and of abiding confidence in God from day to day. So doing, you will go on stedfastly, and with His grace attain final persever-ance, the end and object of all true interior life.

Temptation

"Blessed is the man that endureth temptation."—JAMES i. 12

IT is easy to realise God's Hand shielding and protecting the soul, when all is smooth and comforting; when His peace fills the heart, and neither devil or man disturb it. But when God withdraws His consolations, and suffers His servant to be tried by temptation and assault, it is harder to believe that His Hand is still over the sufferer, and such an one is tempted to ask anxiously what he has done to be thus chastened? But it is an Apostle who tells us that he is blessed who endures temptation, and the Angel Raphael told Tobit that it was because he was acceptable in God's Sight that he was tempted;[1] treating temptation as an actual reward rather than a punishment. Such thoughts will surely strengthen us under the trial.

---

1 " Quia acceptus eras Deo, necesse fuit ut tentatio probaret te." Tob. xii. 13. (The English version does not give this sense to the passage.)

He who gives himself heartily to God may count upon many and varied temptations, and one who through long years underwent no trial or humiliation, might well question the soundness of his position. When we speak of proving a thing, we mean putting its quality, its strength, its reality, to the test. Unproved goodness is but an uncertain matter—"he rides easily whom God carries;" prayer is no hard matter when it is full of sweetness; victory over self costs but little when nature is not greatly thwarted. Holiness would scarce be what it is, rare, hard to win, if it involved no struggles, no difficulties. St. Paul certainly held it to be no light matter when he compared it to the athletes' contest, saying, "Now they do it to attain a corruptible crown, but we an incorruptible." Untried virtue can scarce deserve the name.

To prove, is to purify : as metals are proved and purified in the crucible, so is man's heart proved in the furnace of affliction—the selfishness, the pride which tarnish it are purged away; and without some such process there can be none of that purity and heavenliness which follow upon temptation endured. Purity, faith, trust, come forth with fresh beauty from the pressure of temptation, and when Jesus Himself had borne His hour of temptation, "angels came and ministered to Him." Weariness, heartache, desolation, purify love and kindle courage; the contempt of men extinguishes human respect and self-conceit—all temptations tend to detachment, humility, union with God. Who then will be afraid? If it savours too much of spiritual pride to desire them, at least we need not fear them, or give way to despair at their approach. If you say that you fear to yield under them, I would say, are you not rather shrinking from that vigorous defence, which is to win the "crown of life" promised to him who endures temptation?[1] "Yet is he not crowned, except he strive lawfully;" St. Paul says.[2] Such fear comes because you are looking at the battle as though it were to be fought in your own strength, not in that of God. By yourself, forsooth, you would be soon overthrown, but with the Everlasting Arms around you, what is there to fear? Can men or devils tear you from out their shelter? And He has promised to succour you in the temptations which He sends, and into which you are not thrust by self-will. "God is faithful," says St. Paul, " He will not suffer you to be tempted above that ye are able, but will with the temptation also make a way to escape, that ye may be able to bear it."[3]

[1] James i. 12. [2] 2 Tim. ii. 5. [3] 1 Cor. x. 13.

Faithful to His promises, watching over you in the
struggle, making you a way to escape. Who would
not fight bravely, knowing that His Eye is on them ?
You do not feel His Hand, you say ?   What matters
if you know it is there ?   You are well-nigh certain
that you have yielded to the pressure of temptation ? Do not hastily judge of that—it may be
but a snare of the devil.   Rather let your director
judge, and be satisfied with his judgment.   He will
see more truly than you are able to do, and it is
self-will to persist in your own view.

Temptations vary of course in kind, according to
individual character and circumstance.   The com-
monest class of temptations among ordinary Christians is of a material kind.   These, however, do not
usually beset those who have given themselves
wholly to God, and there is but one way of dealing
with them, namely, a firm resolution to be watchful
and faithful to the leadings of grace in the most
trifling details, guarding, not merely against mortal
sin, and all that can tend to it, but also against
every possible imperfection and frailty.   "Abstain
from all appearance of evil."   Such a course will
put an end to this kind of temptation, which often
arises mainly from a certain lack of decision of will.
God often withholds temptation from beginners, in

order that they may gain strength and solidity; but sooner or later the soul will be tried in some shape—it may be from having given way to self-confidence, or excessive self-contemplation. Thus the devil tries to keep one man from Communion, under the pretext of unfitness or unprofitableness. But this is a purely vague, imaginary fear, and should be disregarded. It would not arise if we were content not to sit in judgment upon the worth of our own Communions. Again, the devil persuades another man that his prayers and meditations are waste of time, because he is harassed with distractions, and has no conscious sweetness in them. But this is mere delusion. No prayer so tends to stifle self-love as that which is dry and even painful. Another common form of temptation sets before us some course of action different to that which God appoints to us. He leads us into silence and retreat, and we persist in rushing into a busy outer life, under the excuse of zeal, good works, and our neighbour's edification. Or we are tempted to doubt the wisdom of the director we are under when his guidance does not tally with our inclination.

Souls that have made further progress in the interior life meet with a different class of temptations, which indeed assume rather a character of

trial than of ordinary temptation. God allows them
to be humbled and purged by violents assaults of
Satan, it may be against their faith, hope, love of
God or man, and they may mistakenly imagine
themselves to be yielding under the pressure. At
such times no one is capable of judging as to his
own spiritual condition ; the right course is to be
perfectly open and true with your director, not
allowing fear or shame to keep back anything ; and
to accept his decisions and guidance as to your
soul's state without any questioning or self-will.
As a general rule, it is well not to fear or foresee
temptation, or attempt to prepare yourself for it,
but rather to rest childlike in God's Arms, trusting
wholly in Him, confident in His assistance. The
only real preparation against temptation is unfailing
co-operation with grace, and heartiness in conquering self; for, after all, the devil's chief strength is
won from our self-love. Then, again, when temptation comes, let it pass over you like a storm cloud,
while you hold fast to God, relaxing nothing o.
your ordinary religious exercises. Thus, supposing
that the most harassing thoughts distract you in
prayer or even at Holy Communion, beware of
leaving off either—" Resist the devil, and he will
flee from you." And when the cloud has passed,

beware of recurring to it with an over-scrupulous inquiry as to the nature of your resistance. That is not the real test of your spiritual state—your habitual conduct is the only thing by which to judge. If you are humble, obedient, diligent in all your duties, and steady in self-denial, God will never allow you to be overcome by temptation, and your confessor will judge of you by these tests. The less you dwell upon your temptations, their tendencies and results, except in order to place yourself faithfully before him, the better.

Self

GOD Alone can speak of Himself as an independent existence, the centre and standard of all things, for He Alone IS ; all else is His creation, the work of His Hand, helpless and worthless in itself. Once accept this principle, and it is easy to feel the unlawfulness of any human self-assertion. Men are wont to weigh themselves, to love, esteem, prize themselves, to lay claim to the love and esteem of others; looking at everything from their own point of view, making their own interest the centre round which everything they do works. They seek self on all sides, as though all creation was destined to their service; they love others only in proportion to their own advantage as derived therefrom ; self-interest or vanity is at the root of everything, even their service performed for God Himself. This earthly self is the root of pride, and consequently of all sin ; it is God's enemy, as well as man's, and if we could banish self, we should banish crime from

the world—men would love one another with all
charity, their hearts and desires would turn unhin-
dered to God, He would be their sole object, peace
and joy would surround us.

There are two shapes assumed by self, the one
is gross and material, the self of worldly men, who
are for ever in pursuit of earthly gain, and of those
who, misled by a delusive intellectual pride, affect to
be superior to common prejudices, and make a law
of their own reason. Nearly all the vices which
degrade mankind and afflict the world are the off-
spring of this grosser self.

But there is another more spiritual self which is
peculiar to religious people, the evil of which it
would not be easy to describe; how it blights and
withers devotion, warping and misdirecting it, and
bringing holiness into contempt and ill-repute. Who
can tell all the meanness, the weakness, the falls to
which it leads; how it fills pious people with fretting scruples, and makes them restless, uneasy, fan-
ciful, capricious, absurd, jealous, censorious, ill-tem-
pered, often intolerable to themselves and others!
Who can say how it hinders and thwarts the work
of grace, and promotes Satan's attempts, how it
weakens us in time of temptation, making us fail
under trial, and grudge giving what God requires

M

of us, how many noble aims it turns aside, how many good works it poisons, how many faults it disguises till we mistake them for virtues.

The spirit of self, whether it take a material or a moral shape, has ever the same result, that of utterly blinding us. We fancy that we see and know ourselves truly, but nothing can be a greater delusion; we will not let our eyes be opened, and are vexed with those who attempt the task. All suggestions and remonstrances are attributed either to unkindness or error; no matter how justly fault is found, wounded self-love is irritable and intolerant of the slightest touch. On the same principle we feel perfectly competent to judge and direct ourselves, and even those whose office it is to direct us. Self-love thinks no director wise who will not soothe and flatter it; and he who requires the submission of our own opinion and will stands a chance of being forsaken as depriving the conscience of liberty. Tell us, when under the influence of this dangerous enemy self, that we must resist it, and conquer our dislikes, try to open our eyes to our pet faults, point out the hollowness of our motives, ask any sacrifice of us, and we start away at once from the intolerable yoke. Excuses without end are at hand; we are misunderstood, it is all exaggeration or mistake, in short everybody is wrong save ourselves. But all the time there can be no real holiness without the destruction of this odious self; all Christian doctrine, all the workings of grace aim at this point. The love of God and of self are as the two opposing scales of the spiritual balance, and if one rises the other must inevitably sink; and there is no other means whereby to attain perfection than a continual war and death to self. But since we are not skilful or brave, or disinterested enough, to wage this war alone, we must needs throw ourselves upon God, and ask Him to fight for us and in us, while we strive in all things to work together with Him.

My chief enemy, the enemy through whom all other foes, the world and the devil, reach me, is myself, the "old man," the "old Adam" of which St. Paul speaks: the self-love which was born with me grew faster than my mental growth, and has been strengthened by my passions, by my natural want of perception, the weakness of my will, the abuse I have made of my freedom, my bad habits and sins. How am I to resist this terrible foe? Where am I to begin? My very efforts to overcome it seem to give it new strength; self-love finds food in everything it contemplates, and admires itself in every attempt I make to conquer a fault or acquire a virtue; it drinks up the praise bestowed upon me, it takes pride even in what I mean to be acts of self-humiliation. It forcibly appropriates what is God's work only, and would fain take His glory for itself. There is no hope save in Him; and He must fight for me. My self-love is His enemy too. He must subdue, crush, destroy it in me, or I can never get the victory. Blessed and All-powerful Lord, I give myself up to Thee, deal with me as Thou wilt. Overrule all my resistance to Thy chastening Hand, punish me when I fail. Cast out from me every shadow of complacency and self-satisfaction, every inclination to think that I can do aught save in Thee. Leave me not, my gracious Saviour, until the old Adam be rooted out, and the new Adam, even Thyself, and Thine own quickening Spirit, take sole possession of me, so that I may be brought to that Home and Rest which Thou hast prepared for them that love Thee. Amen.

The Nothingness of Man

" Mine age is even as nothing in respect of Thee."—Psa. xxxix. 6

WE are not always willing to accept the doctrine of our own nothingness, or of the necessity of a death unto self ; and yet it is a true doctrine, and not really harsh as we may suppose. When God requires such humiliation of self, He only exacts that which is His due, He would only have us realise our true position. Had the taint of original sin never fallen upon man, were we still pure and innocent, we could still be nothing of ourselves ; our very existence is a gift of God, still more all else we possess, and it is mere arrogance to murmur at our own nothingness.

Some will say that it is easy enough to admit our nothingness with respect to God, but less so with respect to men, who are no other than ourselves. No doubt it is easy to confess our nothingness as regards God in words only, but when we come to act upon it, to give Him that which is His

due, to let Him exercise His rights over us, body
and soul, it is not so easy, although He deals ever
so gently with our weakness, and never takes us at
unawares when He proves and tries us.   As regards
men, I grant that they have no inherent right over
us, and that their contempt and oppression is an
injustice ; but we have not any more reason to
murmur because of that, inasmuch as being ourselves naught, we have no right to anything, and
the injustice is done to God, whose law is infringed
by those who oppress or despise us.   The injury is
done to Him, not to me, and I may not retaliate or
give way to a revengeful spirit.   If we could always
keep this truth in view, there would be fewer heart-
burnings and animosities among us, but the endless
dwelling upon our own supposed rights in which we
indulge, while we forget God's rights, is the source
of untold evil.   Doubtless, it is difficult to follow
out this course, but it is possible. God never exacts
what is impossible of us, and He would have us act
both towards Himself and towards our neighbour
as being nought, having nought, claiming nought.
What can God lay upon us beyond our deserts,
more especially if we believe that our temporal
afflictions and humiliations will be " an exceeding
weight of glory" hereafter, and that those who have

been esteemed vile among men shall reign with Christ hereafter? Moreover, Christ Himself has said that His yoke is easy and His burden light; and however burdensome the yoke in itself might be, He always lightens it to those who bear it willingly for His Sake. Love does not put away suffering, but it teaches us to love suffering and to bear it gladly.

The chief pang of most trials is not so much the actual suffering itself, as our own inherent spirit of resistance to it. But a soul which accepts its own nothingness is free from this resistance, and nothing can disturb its peace—the habit of self-renunciation strengthens continually, and we are astonished to find ourselves bearing that which once seemed intolerable, calmly and patiently. It is pride which makes contempt, or censure, or other humiliations, so hard to bear; we would fain be esteemed, well thought of, considered and respected, and when such consideration is denied us, we are excited and irritated. But if we can triumph over pride, throw aside self-esteem, and take all trifling mortifications with an interior spirit of humility, we shall soon cease to care much what is said or thought of us, or even how we are treated. A dead man has no sensitiveness as to praise or blame, and a soul which

is dead to self shares that calm stillness and deep
repose.

In spiritual things, our trials mostly come from a
lack of sufficient self-surrender ; a lurking attempt
to please ourselves, self-complacency, poisons even
our devotions; and hence we are far from indifferent
to dryness or sweetness, we cannot endure any
seeming estrangement from God, we exhaust ourselves in struggles if He hides His Face, and thus
arise discouragement and false alarms.   But it does
not follow that things are really amiss with us because He withholds sensible consolations.   A true
spirit of self-renunciation, which seeks to serve Him
for Himself Alone, will bear with all discomforts,
content to know that He accepts our service, and
convinced that we deserve no more.   All true peace
lies in forgetfulness of self, which can only be found
in God.   Once gain this, and neither earth or hell
will prevail to trouble you, or disturb your rest in
your Lord and His Holy Will.

Generosity

GENEROSITY is of two kinds, natural and supernatural; both are the gift of God, and the former begets the latter. He who seeks to tread the paths of holiness with stedfast perseverance, needs a large supply of this grace to meet the perpetual sacrifices which it involves; and you may observe that all those who bear the stamp of God's Saints are to be distinguished by an elevated tone which is not of this world, as well as by a special sensitiveness to the sorrows of others. A high tone of feeling and a tender heart, are the sources whence generosity springs, and no grovelling soul, which is indifferent to a brother's woe, can attain to it, or really give God that " offering of a free spirit" which is so precious in His Sight. Still, though natural generosity has a direct tendency to that which is supernatural, they are by no means one and the same. Earthly generosity consists in sharing what we possess with others; spiritual generosity implies giving to God, not only all we have, but all that we are; it implies the sacrifice of mind, will, health, reputation, life, in short, of all that constitutes that subtle self in which our natural affections are centred. St. Gregory says that it is easy to give up what a man has, but very hard to give up himself;[1] and in truth it cannot be done save through the grace of God. We are tempted to think we have achieved the work, when in our first fervours we have given ourselves heartily to God, and made strong protestations of our readiness to bear all things for love of Him. Yet this is but the first step, and the real sacrifice is altogether another matter.

When God leads the soul into the path of true sacrifice, He generally withdraws sensible consolations, and permits repugnance, revulsion, a general rising of self-love, to try it. At such a time we are apt to experience a vehement opposition within ourselves to God's Will, and the interior struggle is often a very agony—we cry out for the cup to pass from us—the whole natural self resists that destruction which threatens it. But meanwhile

---

1 " Et fortasse laboriosum non est homini relinquere sua; sed valde laboriosum est relinquere semetipsum."—Hom. xxiii. in Evang.

God's grace confirms the will and carries it through these hours of suffering. Or it may be that at first the soul is strong to bear its trial, and then grows weary and restless, and frets under the struggle. Why, we may ask, does God permit all this? In the first place, He would teach us to know our weakness and worthlessness, lest we should yield to self-complacency, and attribute such sacrifices as we are able to make to our own strength. We learn, amid our trouble, to prize the upholding grace of God more duly, and such struggles are among our best lessons in the difficult paths of the interior life.

There is always some taint of self in mere natural generosity—interested motives, pride and vanity intrude, a love of patronising, the praise of men, or even our own conscious self-applause find a part therein. But none of these can reach supernatural generosity—self-love can find nothing to feed upon in that, the very aim of which is its destruction. Our own interests are sacrificed to those of God; our victories are too hardly won to excite any vanity—interior and exterior humiliations avert human praise, and the pride which attends it; all is for God, and Him Only. So when He demands some great sacrifice of His child, He supplies a

proportionate generosity of spirit, kindling and
exalting the soul till it is filled with a boundless
desire for self-devotion, and in the power of His
Grace weakness is made strong. He who once felt
God's ordinary law, still more His Counsels, hard
to fulfil, now finds nothing hard. "I will run the
way of Thy Commandments when Thou hast set
my heart at liberty."   Where he stumbled and
toiled wearily, when carrying an earthly heart, he
now runs freely and joyfully, because God's touch
has enlarged and expanded his heart.[1] Our progress in His service depends upon the heartiness
with which we give ourselves up to it ; and what
seems a great matter to a niggardly self-seeking
soul will be as nothing to one who has lost self in
God.   But such a " free spirit " must be the subject
of constant prayer.   Ask that you may never
measure your service by your own narrow earthly
notions.   It is a marvellous thing, in truth, to
serve God, and we are powerless to do it save
through His Grace. He must take away from
us the spirit of self, and fill us with His Own
Spirit, before we can hope to succeed. The less
we live according to our own imaginations, the

[1] In the Vulgate the rendering is, " Viam mandatorum Tuorum
cucurri, quum *dilatasti* cor meum."

more we shall live to God. " His ways are not
as our ways, or His thoughts as our thoughts."
Be it ours—

> " To lose ourselves,
> And find ourselves in God."

Simplicity

IT is not easy to define simplicity, and yet it is the source and fulfilment of God's Perfections, and of all perfection in the interior life. God's Attributes are all stamped with it—Eternal, without beginning or end, indivisible—HE IS. The more our souls can approach to such simplicity, the nearer they are to Him in whose Image and Likeness they were created, and the more all sinks before that one thing, Love of God,—as the object of their single affection, intellect and will, the more the aim of all spiritual training, union with Him, is attained. A simple heart will love all that is most precious on earth, husband or wife, parent or child, brother or friend in God, without marring its singleness: external things will have no attraction save inasmuch as they lead souls to Him; all exaggeration, unreality, affectation and falsehood must pass away from such an one, as the dews dry up before the sunshine. The single motive is to please God, and hence arises total indifference as to what others will say and think, so that words and actions are perfectly simple and natural, as in His Sight only. Such Christian simplicity is the very perfection of the interior life—God, His will and pleasure its sole object.

But the world's spirit—"which lieth in wickedness "[1]—is far otherwise, and it despises and rejects all such singleness of heart. Its deals in dissimulation and unreality, self-seeking, earthly gain, and it "counts their life madness" who do otherwise. There is and must be a ceaseless opposition between the two. At the same time, remember that it is of the very essence of such Christian simplicity to be unknown of men. Those who are blessed with it will always avoid all that attracts remark, they will not affect any singular ways or noticeable habits ;—their holiness is interior, hidden not only from others, but from themselves; God would have them all His own, He hides them under the shadow of His Wings, and the more completely to secure this great grace of a hidden life, He often permits them to be despised, humbled, and persecuted by men, even as was their Lord Himself.

[1] 1 John v. 19.

Obedience

OBEDIENCE costs the human spirit a higher
price than any other virtue. It is easier to
bear fasts and austerities than to submit one's will
to that of another. Obedience comes into direct
collision with the very essence of self-love, and with
that side of it which seems reasonable and justifi-
able. Why should I not judge for myself according
to my own lights, and only follow the opinion of
other men where it seems good to me to do so?
What can be more intolerable than to give another
control over my conduct, over the secrets of my
inner life? It is a great sacrifice, but it is one
which affects our heavenly life, and our eternal
happiness: it is a means by which God sets forward
our perfection. "Behold, to obey is better than
sacrifice, and to hearken than the fat of rams."[1]
But, you will say, that applies to obeying God, and
if I do that, why need I obey men? Is not His

[1] 1 Sam. xv. 22.

law, His grace sufficient for me? Nevertheless, all
authority comes from Him, and it is the ordering
of His Providence that in things spiritual as in
things temporal, we should submit to those He has
set over us. "Obey them that have the rule over
you, and submit yourselves, for they watch for your
souls as they that must give account, that they
may do it with joy, and not with grief, for that is
unprofitable for you."[1] Those who would shake off
this law, do so at the great peril of their souls.

But, you reply, why must I obey a man who
may fall into error himself, and mislead me? The
spiritual guide to whom you submit, is sent by God
to lead you in the way of holiness, and if you obey
him heartily for God's Sake, you may trust to God,
confident that He will inspire His servant with
whatever wisdom is needful for your guidance. Of
course I am presupposing that you have put yourself under a director whose faith, piety, and discre-
tion are unquestionable, and if so, have no fears ;
God will not allow him to make any essential mistakes in guiding you, and His Grace will make up
for any minor imperfections, and cause them to
work for good both to you and him. Such a broad
foundation is necessary for all real obedience, or it

[1] Heb. xiii. 17.

N

would not withstand the trials and temptations to which it is liable.   Remember too that obedience gives a value to little things, as well as to those that are greater ; wherever God sees your will set aside, He sees you striving to fulfil His Own, and that is infinitely acceptable to Him.   Obedience strengthens the soul against Satan's assaults.   Our Dear Lord Himself, "though He were a Son, yet learned obedience by the things which He suffered,"[1] and became obedient unto death,"[2] and if He is our model, we need not shrink through pride or self-sufficiency from treading in His steps. Our obedience will never reach as far as His. From His Birth to His Death He never "pleased Himself."   Of which of us can the like ever be said?

[1] Heb. v. 8.   [2] Phil. ii. 8.

Humility

" Learn of Me, for I am meek and lowly in heart, and ye shall find
rest unto your souls."—MATT. x. 29

MEEKNESS is the result of true humility.
He who is lowly in heart will inevitably be
meek, and he who is deficient in meekness, is sure
to be deficient also in humility. Never was there
humility like to that of Jesus Christ, voluntary,
deep, practical; taking upon Him man's nature,
bearing all that is most despised of men:—we cannot be humble in like manner; nothing to begin
with, we cannot go lower;—sinners, meriting God's
sentence, how can we humble ourselves below our
natural condition ? Yet pride springs up on all
sides, and makes it well nigh intolerable when the
faintest shadow of contempt or neglect falls across
our path from God or man. We are disturbed,
disgusted, beside ourselves often with vexation, at
the very thought of being despised, instead of
counting it as no more than our due. How carefully we avoid all that can lower us in men's

esteem, sacrificing duty and conscience to the dread of ridicule, or the worthless opinion of the world. How often we break promises and resolutions solemnly made before God, in order to appear something which we are not, in the world's eye— and too often we rather pride ourselves upon our worldly wisdom, and think lightly of that love of humiliation which God's chosen saints have felt, but which is so far from us. Real humility would take no count of any natural advantages, whether birth, intellect, beauty, wealth, or whatsoever they be. They are not our own work, and God does not give such gifts to nourish pride and vanity. Of themselves they are not profitable to our salvation; —it may be that through misuse we have turned them into occasions of sin, and far from glorying in them, perhaps they ought to deepen our humility. Real humility would hold itself unworthy of the praise of men, and would refer all such to God, while it would accept blame and contempt as its natural portion ; even welcoming it, and not struggling to justify itself in the world's esteem. Real humility serves God in a disinterested spirit, which owns that it deserves nothing; accepting His gifts thankfully, but so far from appropriating them, as to be rather humbled by

them.[1]   It is never surprised or discouraged at being unsuccessful, but, like the Canaanitish woman,
is content to gather up the crumbs which fall from
its Master's table.   When God's Face seems averted,
it is ready to cry out with the prophet, "I will
bear the indignation of the Lord, because I have
sinned against Him."[2]   Whatever visitations come
from God or man, true humility takes them as its
due, only asking strength to bear them; and thence
arise peace and blessing.

How can such humility be attained?   By entire
self-abandonment in God's Hands, by giving ourselves unreservedly to Him ; He will work out His
Will in us, and supply all we need to co-operate
with Him.   He will fill us with that deep, generous,
restful, unchangeable humility which, while it lowers
us as sinners to the very depths, yet raises us above
the world, the devil and ourselves, through His own
untold Strength and Holiness.   But this humility is
not of us—it is His work only—it is the fruit of temptation, suffering, and trial; and those who have it,
know it least.   No Saint of God ever yet believed
himself to be humble ; the vision would destroy the
reality.

[1] " Humbled by all He gives,
Thankful for what He takes away."
[2] Mic. vii. 9.

On the Right Use of Time

THE greater number of men use their time amiss; many others are perplexed how to use it, or rather how to get rid of it; their only object is to dispose of time as pleasantly as may be. Such people are not usually very successful; a frivolous, idle use of time makes men weary of themselves and of life, but the habit of wasting time is unfortunately more easily acquired than set aside. Nevertheless a day will come when the abuse of this gift will be a matter of sore regret to all who have failed to use it as a trust from God, to be returned to Him with usury.

Surely any one aiming at an interior life must be disposed to ask himself what time really is as regards himself? It is his present, actual existence. Past time is nothing to him, he cannot recall it or alter its character. Time to come is nothing to him now, and may never be his; no one can count certainly upon another hour of time. The only

portion of time on which we can reckon is that
actually present—the actual moment in which we
live, which itself passes away so rapidly that no
earthly process of thought or power can stay it.
All these are commonplace truths, which every one
knows, yet how few act upon them. Whence comes
this actual moment of time and existence? It is
God's gift; He gave you being, He has brought
you hitherto through time, He gives you the
minute now fleeting by ; but neither you or any
other human being knows whether He will give
you the next. But you must go on to ask, Why
He has given you this gift of time? That you
may attain a blessed eternity. Faith and reason
alike tell you that your soul will live for ever, and
God has filled your heart with a craving for immortality which will not be disappointed. But eternity
may be happy or miserable, and that according to
the use made here of time. If hitherto you have
misused it, begin at once to do differently, win the
grace of final perseverance, and when time ceases
to be for you, an eternity of happiness will begin ;
but if death surprises you while still failing to use
time rightly, what can you look for but an eternity
of wretchedness? If then you grant that your
future life depends upon the right use of time, and

that you cannot influence either that which is past
or that which is to come, surely the practical result
is that your whole eternity depends upon the
moments now actually passing. And if so, there
can be no question more imminently concerning
your welfare, than this, What is your condition
now? Are you fit to die at this moment? And
if not, is it not worse than madness to rest satisfied,
and count on the future, when in fact you cannot
be sure of a single hour?

All the events of life, sin only excepted, work
together for your future blessedness. Sin alone
can destroy it ; and sin is the work of a moment of
time. Directly that your will assents to sin, your
soul is in peril, whether you accomplish the sinful
act or not, and if death surprises you while thus
consenting to sin, you are lost. But how can you
be sure that death will not come while you are
admitting the first inroad of a sinful thought? And
if so, of what untold importance those passing
moments in which it arises are? All temporal evils
may be turned to good, if met in the Spirit of
Christ's Gospel—there is no need to fear them so
boundlessly as we sometimes do—sin is the only
evil which reaches to eternity, and for which we
cannot be certain of a remedy, since repentance is

the only remedy for sin, and that may not be within
our power. Such thoughts as these would surely
guide you to resolve never to do anything which
risks your eternity of bliss—to use every moment as
God would have you, with a view to that eternity—
never to delay what you can and ought to do now,
to a season which may never be given you—never
to waste moments which are so infinitely important
in questionable, or hurtful occupations ; and to
consider frequently that a life which has so weighty
an object, and which may end at any moment,
should be carefully used, given to God and the
duties of your position. Some such rules as these
ought to be followed by all who call themselves
Christians. But those who seek to live an interior
life should do more ; their time is in no sense their
own—it is God's only, and they must seek to rule
every instant of time, whether given to duty or to
innocent recreation, according to His direct Will.
Nor will such a habit of life be an irksome restraint
—they will live as children beneath a Father's Eye,
tasting a blessed freedom which comes only with a
service of love.

The only way to attain this is by a spirit of recollection which ever watches to learn what God
requires, and hastens to fulfil His Will, so soon as

it is perceived. This habit will stamp the whole
life, and amid whatever exterior duties surround
you, you will hold fast to God ; nor will you be
restless and disturbed as to whether you are using
your time rightly, because you will feel that He is
guiding you. The interior life has but one object
—to glorify and love God—to glorify Him in
every action and suffering, accepting all things
at His Hand ; and to love Him, not in mere
formal acts or deliberate expressions, but with
a continual practical devotion which rests itself
wholly in His Hands. This mental attitude
colours the soul's life—your external circumstances may change, toil may take the place
of rest, sickness of health, trials may thicken
within and without. Externally, you are the
prey of such circumstances, but if your heart is
stayed on God, no changes or chances can touch
it, and all that may befall you will but draw you
closer to Him. In that respect time already is
blended with eternity to your soul, and whatever
the present moment may bring, your knowledge
that it is His Will, and that your future heavenly
life will be influenced by it, will make all not only
tolerable, but welcome to you, while no vicissitudes
can affect you greatly, knowing that He Who holds

you in His Powerful Hand, cannot change, but abideth for ever. Happy they who measure time and its use as in His Sight, happier still if they live according to their knowledge!

The Blindness of Man

" For judgment I am come into this world, that they which see not might see, and that they which see might be made blind."—JOHN ix. 39.

OUR Lord spake these words in connection with the restoration of one blind from his birth, to whom He had given sight both bodily and spiritual; the Pharisees, who were looking on, being unable to read the mystery right. But the meaning of the Saviour's words reaches us all. We are all born in the blindness of original sin, knowing neither God or ourselves, wholly ignorant as to the things which concern us most, our true happiness, and the way by which to attain it. We are blind and we know it not, we never should have realised our darkness, unless God had become man in order to give us light. But the worst of all is when men think they see, notwithstanding they are blind—as it was with the heathen, the Scribes and Pharisees. Now though Christi-

anity has shed its light upon us, it has not altogether dispelled our darkness ; where self-love and
self-will linger, there we shall ever be blind as concerns God and ourselves ; we fail to perceive His
Ways, we misapprehend true holiness ; and we are
deceived as to our own faults though clear-sighted
enough as to those of our neighbour's. The soul
that is blinded thus does not and cannot know itself; but God's Light quickly opens the eyes which
are not wilfully closed.   There is a wilful blindness,
which refuses to confess that it cannot see, and how
should that Divine Light avail those who say, "We
see," and "whose sin remaineth ?"   How can it
penetrate those self-willed, obstinate minds, which
cling to their own prejudices, and persist in seeing
everything according to their own light ?   Yet this
blindness is by no means uncommon even in religious
people, and inasmuch as it springs from pride, it
hinders grace with a persistency which nothing save
humiliation can overcome.   Our Dear Lord, the
Light of the World, came with the intent of healing our blindness, but He said Himself that He
came "that they which see not might see, and that
they which see might be made blind."   What did
these words mean ?   Do any see of themselves
without His Light ?   In truth no.   But whereas

some see their own infirmity in all lowliness by the
light of His Grace, and seek to be healed of Him,
and on these He sheds the fulness of His Blessed
Light; there are others who deny that they are
blind, and persist in remaining in darkness. It may
be that they ascribe the light He gives them to their
own merits, and He punishes them by withdrawing
it; or they misuse and neglect that light, and will
not walk by it, and it ceases to visit their eyes. To
which of these classes do you belong? Woe be to
any of us who cleaves to his own light, and chooses
his own path; God will surely leave us to our own
blind guidance, and how shall we escape a fall?
Nor less great is the danger, if we mistake His light
for our own, and feed presumption and vanity
thereby; or if we fail to use the light God sends
according to His Will. If we reject it, He will take
it from us, and give it to those who will use it
better. There is but one safe course; to imitate
the blind man near Jericho, who cried out, "Jesus,
Thou Son of David, have mercy on me;" and when
Jesus asked him, "What wilt thou that I shall do
unto thee?" he said, "Lord, that I may receive my
sight."[1] How Thou wilt, dear Lord, only grant
that I may see!

[1] Luke xviii.

If you are called upon to make some important
decision, mistrust self,—mistrust the natural instincts, your excitable passions, impulses, prejudices,
your human respect, and humbly ask God to enlighten you, to shew you the right way, and give
you courage to follow it. Wait ever upon His
Light, fearing to stumble if you lose it for but a
moment. Further, give Him constant thanks for
His Light, confessing that all light comes of Him.[1]
Do not trust in your own spiritual perceptions, or
your mental powers—" The things of God are perceived by the Spirit of God." He delights to enlighten the simple-hearted, who realise their own
ignorance, and see no good thing in themselves,
but refer all to God. Oh! if men could but grasp
the knowledge that self-esteem is the most treacherous of foes, that God's Will is to humble and crush
it, they would never rest till they had trodden it
down ; they would rejoice to have no independent
being, but in all things to wait upon Him ; to keep
their hearts ever ready to receive the inspirations of
His Grace. Do not fear to see your own weakness.
and poverty by the Light of that Grace, it will
shew you your faults, and give you power to con-

1 " As every lovely hue is light,
So every light is Love."

quer them.　Do not seek to shatter the mirror
which reflects your soul's lack of beauty ; rather
welcome the truth, and believe that next to the
knowledge of God, nothing is so precious as the
knowledge of self.　Without it, you can scarce hope
to reach to His knowledge.　These are the "deeps
which call one to another;"[1] God's Power and
man's weakness.　Let us cry out with St. Augustine,
"Lord, teach me to know Thee, and to know myself!"

[1] Psa. xlii. 9.

The Weakness and Corruption of Man's Heart

NOT only is man's understanding blind, his heart is weak and corrupt—weak, that is, as regards what is good — unhappily he rarely lacks force when it is a question of evil. Yet God made man "very good," and it is through sin only that we have been thus perverted. Original sin has reversed the order of God's creation : He gave man a heart which tended to love Him above all else, but sin has taught us self-love, and that self-love does not seek what alone would bring happiness, but rather draws us down to earthly things, which blind us to those which are heavenly. It is the same all through life, the wants, the enjoyments of our bodies engross us, to the exclusion of higher aims ; — the Saints have confessed and mourned over this infirmity, but worldly men heed it not,— rather despising those who would fain conquer earthly passions, for the sake of a treasure not

o

made with hands. The whole Christian law aims
at uprooting this worldly spirit; and at times we
open our eyes to the beauty of holiness,—we make
good resolutions, and fondly imagine ourselves
firmly set upon our heavenward path; but too
often the least hindrance throws us back, some
trifling earthly lure makes us forget all we had
resolved, and we fall helplessly.   Well may we cry
out with St. Paul, "the good that I would I do not,
but the evil which I would not that I do."

Even that measure of "willing good" which we
possess is the work of grace only, not any merit
of our own,—passion and inclination are almost
always on the wrong side; our perversity frets
against God's restraining Hand, and in many cases
men abstain from sin rather out of fear of human
law than that of God.   Nay more, sin has a
positive attraction for us, and as St. Paul tells us,
the very prohibitions of the law kindle a desire for
that which is forbidden.   Who does not know the
irresistible desire most people experience to read a
forbidden book, or to see a forbidden sight?   The
moment some secret is kept back from us, we are
bent upon its discovery; we fret after some unattainable possession, regardless of all God grants
us—in short the natural man kicks and frets against

all law, all restraint. But for the check put upon us by religion, and by God's Grace, there is nothing of which we should not be capable. As St. Augustine says, we are capable of every sin that we have seen our neighbour commit, unless God's Grace restrain us.

Such thoughts would be appalling, if God unveiled them to us suddenly;—He rather leads us gradually to the self-knowledge which is essential to humility and watchfulness, and with the deeper perception of our own proneness to fall, He quickens in us the fulness of that gracious promise, " My Grace is sufficient for thee, for My Strength is made perfect in weakness."[1] If the great Apostle was in danger of being " exalted above measure through the abundance of revelations," so that he needed "a thorn in the flesh, the messenger of Satan to buffet him," how much more such as we are ?

[1] 2 Cor. xii. 9.

Detachment

A HOLY man of old summed up the interior
life in three words, Flight, Silence, Rest.
Flight from all that would lead the soul from God;
—Silence internal and external, that it may hear His
Voice;—Rest of the heart and mind in Him. All
who are called to an interior life are not called,
like St. Arsenius, to a literal flight from the world,
but they are called to "use as not abusing it;"—
to seek ever increasing detachment from it and
from all that tends to separate them from God.
At first this may seem no such great thing to de-
mand of a really religious man; but it is harder
than it seems. He must not only fly from sin and
every occasion of sin, but he must shun all those
things which drag him down from his higher aims;
curiosity, self-complacency, the love of praise, a
desire to be of importance, all those trifles which
distract the soul, and fix it upon earthly things.
We need more watchfulness in this respect than it
is our wont to give, for these external matters are

the source of most men's predominant faults, and their great hindrance in the spiritual life.

The chief difficulty in attaining true detachment arises from our natural inclination to throw ourselves into the things of this world, and clinging to them, to seek a rest therein which they can never give. Then comes the hindrance of self-love, and our inordinate desire to be loved and well thought of by others, which leads us to love and seek the things they care for, to frame our thoughts, words and actions upon theirs, till we too often sacrifice God's law and that of our own conscience to the artificial code of the world. Human respect, and the dread of ridicule, hinder many a man from stedfastly asserting the claims of God's precepts as opposed to the world's maxims. It is hard work, no doubt, and can only be accomplished by sitting as loosely as possible to worldly ways, avoiding its bondage as far as possible, refraining from many pleasant things, often restraining one's self in conversation, and when occasion arises asserting the truth of Christ regardless of all human respect, remembering our Saviour's words, "Whosoever shall deny Me before men, him will I also deny before My Father Which is in Heaven."[1]

[1] Matt. x. 33.

Then as to silence; it is a mistake to suppose
that silence is a virtue appertaining solely to the
cloister.   It is more or less a necessity to all interior
life, and when our Lord spoke of the account men
must one day give for " every idle word," He
assuredly did not limit the warning to its walls.
An unrestrained flow of talk is a sure sign of a
trifling dissipated mind; and no one can turn readily
from useless frivolous conversation to recollected
prayer, or spiritual reading, so as to profit by them.
But there is another kind of silence to be cultivated,
besides that of the tongue as regards others.   I
mean silence as regards one's self—restraining the
imagination, not permitting it to dwell overmuch
on what we have heard or said, not indulging in the
phantasmagoria of picture-thoughts, whether of
the past or future.   How hard this is those only
who have struggled with the difficulty know! and
yet how necessary it is, for how can we hope to
hear God's Voice amid the invisible but no less
real whirl of moral dissipation which such a mental
habit induces?   How can we gather those wandering thoughts into a recollected attitude of prayer?
Be sure that you have made no small progress in
the spiritual life, when you can control your imagination, so as to fix it on the duty and occupation

actually existing, to the exclusion of the crowd of thoughts which are perpetually sweeping across the mind. No doubt you cannot prevent those thoughts from arising, but you can prevent yourself from dwelling on them ; you can put them aside, you can check the self-complacency, or irritation, or earthly longings which feed them, and by the practice of such interior mortification you will attain that spirit of inward silence which draws the soul into a close intercourse with God.

Further, you must find rest for your mind and heart in God, and there is no other true rest. But it is not to be found by eagerness, or excitement, or hurry. You will find that blessed rest in proportion as you put aside all agitation, all over eagerness and activity, leaving God to work in you. He is always active, but always at rest, and the soul which cleaves to Him will share His action and His rest alike. It will labour, but so calmly, as scarcely to be conscious of what it does; it moves beneath the guiding Power of God, as we have seen a little child learning to write, and leaving its teacher to direct its hand—going all wrong directly that it makes a voluntary movement. Rest does not mean idleness; the soul which rests in God never ceases its activity, but that activity is always spiritual,

often unconscious.   In ordinary material life, you
look around, you speak, you move, without any
deliberate act of conscious will; and so in the
spiritual life, you pray without a deliberate intention to pray, you rest in God without telling yourself that you are so resting.   But the fact is no less
true, and the very essence of prayer is to lose one's
self in God, which can never be while the soul is
gauging and testing itself.   "Father, into Thy
Hands I commend my spirit," may well be our cry
in this as in all else.   Do with me as Thou wilt in
time and in eternity.   "Whosoever will save his life
shall lose it; and whosoever will lose his life for My
Sake shall find it."[1]

[1] Matt. xvi. 25.

Little Things

"WHOSO despiseth small things shall fall by little things;" and "He that is faithful in that which is least is faithful also in much; and he that is unjust in the least is unjust also in much." Carelessness in trifles leads to grievous falls, and our faithfulness in small duties is a sure test of holiness in purpose and life. But when we speak thus, bear in mind that nothing is small or great in God's Sight; whatever He wills becomes great to us, however seemingly trifling, and if once the voice of conscience tells us that He requires anything of us, we have no right to measure its importance. On the other hand, whatever He would not have us do, however important we may think it, is as nought to us. There is no standard of things great and small to a Christian, save God's Will.

So with respect to our own growth in holiness; our Christian perfection, our very salvation may depend upon something which seems to us a mere trifle. We cannot follow God's secret dealings, or know the consequences of what we are tempted to consider unimportant. Yet how do you know what you may lose by neglecting this duty, which you think so trifling, or the blessing which its faithful performance may bring? Great things, great opportunities of serving God come but rarely, whereas little things whereby our faithfulness is proved occur perpetually. If you wait for some great thing wherein to shew your love to God, you may perchance wait all your life. Besides, great undertakings require great strength, and how can you be sure that you are capable of any such, if you have not been trained and proved by that which is less? Great works imply proportionately great grace, but God does not give His extraordinary gifts of grace, save to those who have made good use of His lesser graces. Then, again, humility esteems all great things above its reach, and clings gladly to lowlier attempts. Be sure that if you do your very best in that which is laid upon you daily, you will not be left without sufficient help when some weightier occasion arises. A desire for great things is generally a delusion of self-love and presumption. Do you wish to practise great austerities and bear heavy crosses in imitation of some saint of God?

Beware of pride and self-esteem ; the saints never conceived any such desires. You will probably grow slack as soon as the first excitement is past, and in spite of all your ambition, you will very likely break down under some little cross which you had despised. It is better to wish for nothing, to choose nothing, to take things as God sends them, and when He sends them, not counting on your own strength and capacity as equal to the smallest undertakings, but believing truly that without His upholding grace you could not stir one step.

There is more effort, more stedfastness, involved in a diligent attention to little duties, than appears at first sight, and that because of their continual recurrence. Such heed to little things implies a perpetual mortification of self, a ceaseless listening to the whispers of grace, a strict watchfulness against every thought, wish, word or act which can offend God ever so little, a constant effort to do everything as perfectly as possible. In truth, it seems to me that he who attains to all this has made some progress in holiness ! Self is always a very real danger in doing or bearing great things for God ; we are apt to admire our own perform-ances, to indulge self-complacency, to esteem our-selves above other men. But little things involve no such risk, self-love finds no pasture in them, and we are not tempted to compare ourselves with others, consequently we are far more likely to go on steadily, and make true progress in a holy life. Little things destroy self by a succession of tiny blows, which do more in their continual pressure than such as are sharper, but rarer; and self-love had better be put to a slow, certain death, than merely scotched, to spring up again with tenacious life. In the beginnings of self-devotion, God sometimes deals some severe blows to self-love, but He generally extinguishes it by a slow, well-nigh invisible process.

Devoted earthly love thinks nothing too trifling, which can give pleasure or pain to the beloved one —and God's jealous, sensitive Love is surely not less than that of men. Who that loves can bear to cast a shadow on the loved face, or cause a sigh to pass his lips? how much less can a loving heart grieve God in anything? how can it bear to forego the tender returns of love He pours on those who are wholly His? All this, however, must be done with a free, childlike spirit, without restlessness and anxiety. He does not ask a fretted, shrinking service. Give yourself to Him, trust Him, fix your eye upon Him, listen to His Voice, and then go on bravely and cheerfully, never doubting for an instant that His grace will lead you in small things as well as great, and will keep you from offending His law of love.

The Use to be Made of our Faults

THIS is a very important point in the spiritual
life; God intends even our faults to set forward the sanctification of our souls, and it rests
with ourselves whether they do so or not. Not un-
frequently we suffer less real injury from a fault itself,
than from the way in which we deal with it. I
am not now speaking of people who give themselves
grudgingly to God, and so commit numberless deliberate faults, which can in no way be turned to
good account. The souls to which I refer are those
who, in spite of all their resolutions against sin, are
continually committing faults through impetuosity,
weakness, or inadvertence. Such people are wont
to be greatly surprised and troubled at their faults;
they give way to false shame, and become fretful
and disheartened. But these are so many signs of
self-love, more hurtful to the soul than the original
fault. You are surprised at your imperfections—
why? I should infer from that, that your self-

knowledge is small. Surely you might rather be astonished that you do not fall into more frequent and more grievous faults, and thank God for His upholding grace. You are worried when you detect a fault, you lose your inward peace, and your disturbance lasts hours or days, as the case may be. This is not right. You should never allow yourself to be disturbed, but when fallen you should rise up quietly, turn with a loving heart to God for forgiveness, and put away the thought of your fault until the proper time comes for self-accusation. Even then, if you should forget it in confession, do not be disturbed.

False shame is another besetting evil; perhaps you are almost afraid to tell your confessor of your faults. You are for ever saying to yourself, "What will he think of me, after all my promises and resolutions?" But if you tell him everything, simply and humbly, he will think all the better of you; if he sees that it costs you a severe struggle, he may not improbably attribute your reluctance to pride; and if he sees that you are not quite open with him, he will not have full confidence in you.

The worst evil, however, is when we grow vexed at our faults; as St. François de Sales says, "We

are angry because we have been angry; impatient
at having shewn impatience. But this is sorry work,
and if you will be honest with yourself, you will see
that it is altogether pride; you are mortified to find
yourself weaker, less holy than you fancied yourself
to be; perhaps too your aim was self-satisfaction,
you wanted to be able to congratulate yourself on
having spent a day or a week free from faults.
Then you grow discouraged, you relax your devotional exercises, and begin to look upon perfection
as unattainable." "What is the use of such perpetual self-restraint and watchfulness?" you ask;
"What good does all my recollection and mortification do me, if none of my faults are corrected,
and I grow no better?" This is neither more or
less than a snare of the devil, and if you would
escape it, you must resolve not to be disheartened,
but even if you were to fall a hundred times a day,
determine to rise up each time, and go onwards.
What will it matter though you have fallen by the
way, if you reach your journey's end safely at last?
God will forgive the falls: they often are caused by
undue haste, which prevents us from taking fitting
precautions, or with timid souls from a perpetual
looking round for imaginary dangers which causes
them to stumble. Perhaps the holiest men are not

always those who commit the fewest faults, but those who have most courage, most love and the most free spirit; those who make the heartiest efforts for conquering self, and who are not afraid of a stumble, even of a fall, so long as their progress is certain. St. Paul says that "all things work together for good to them that love God;" and we may be sure that even their faults are included. God permits them, to cure our vain presumption, and to teach us our true measure. It was so with David. "It is good for me that I have been in trouble, that I may learn Thy statutes." St. Peter fell before he learnt to know his own weakness: St. Paul remained humble amid the triumphs granted to his eloquence; remembering that he had been "a blasphemer, a persecutor, and injurious," he proclaimed himself the "chief of sinners;" bearing a "thorn in the flesh,"—all his days, "lest I should be exalted above measure." Who can doubt that in like manner God will help us to use our daily faults for greater sanctification? All the masters of the spiritual life have observed that God often permits the holiest men to retain certain defects, never wholly overcome, in order to teach them how weak they are without His grace, to check any pride because of His gifts, to destroy the

P

lurking remains of vanity which beset the soul, to keep up constant watchfulness, dependence on God, and unfailing prayer.   The little child who falls as he is learning to walk, clasps tighter hold of his mother after he has hurt himself.

Then, too, our faults sometimes lead to opportunities of good which would not else have arisen. Some outbreak of temper or harshness, or impatience, leads you to humble yourself in reparation. The fault was sudden and not premeditated ;—the reparation is deliberate and hearty, though it costs you no small effort.   Hence it is more acceptable to God than the fault was displeasing.   Again, He sometimes veils real holiness under external imperfections, which most readily meet the eye of our neighbour, so as to prevent the praise of men from tarnishing humility.   God is a mighty Master of souls, be it ours to let Him work His way in us. By all means let it be your great object never to offend Him in anything, but when you have committed a fault, strive to be sorry, not for your mortified pride, but because you have displeased Him; accept all inevitable humiliation, ask God to turn it to His Glory, and you will make greater progress in holiness, than by the most precise and outwardly well regulated life, if it leads to vanity and self-love.

If God requires anything of us, we have no right to draw back under the pretext that we are liable to commit some fault in obeying. It is better to obey imperfectly than not at all. Perhaps you ought to rebuke some one dependent on you, but you are silent for fear of giving way to vehemence; —or you avoid the society of certain persons, because they make you cross and impatient. How are you to attain self-control, if you shun all occasions of practising it ? Is not such self-choosing a greater fault than those into which you fear to fall? Aim at a steady mind to do right, go wherever duty calls you, and believe firmly that God is an indulgent Father, and will forgive the faults which take our weakness by surprise in spite of our sincere desire to please Him.

Direction

DIRECTION and confession should not be considered as separate things. The confessor hears your sins, and absolves them, he prescribes the course by which you can avoid falling anew, and he leads you on towards holiness by the help of ghostly counsel and advice. Surely this is direction, and a good confessor feels that his office includes teaching his penitents how to avoid sin, as well as receiving the confession of sins already committed.

By direction, we mean leading a soul in the paths of holiness, teaching a man to listen for God's Voice, and obey its call, suggesting the means best calculated for avoiding pressing temptations, and for advancing towards perfection,—in a word, direction means guiding the soul to God. This is what St. Gregory meant when he called it "the art of arts."[1] The director must be God's instrument, the channel of the Holy Spirit's grace; and to that end he must lead an interior life, he must be given to

[1] "Ars est artium regimen animarum." Reg. Pastor. i. 1.

prayer, well versed in spiritual things, and that more experimentally than by mere study; he must be free from all personal motives—self-interest and vanity; intent solely on God's Glory and the good of souls; lowly in his own eyes, "weighing the things of God by the Spirit of God." Need I say, such men are rare! Then as to those who receive direction, it will avail them little if they are not docile, obedient, simple-hearted, straightforward, ready to do all that can be asked of them for God, anxious to die to themselves that they may live to Him. If good directors are rare, so are good subjects for direction! Too many of us want to be directed after our own fashion, and would fain combine the double service against which our Lord has warned us—that of God and the world.

He who really desires to give himself to God, should weigh well that direction is a necessity, because the best and wisest men are blinded as to their own inward life, and the holiest and best fitted to direct others would not affect to direct themselves. Humility and the destruction of self-will are indispensable to an interior life, and these are scarcely attainable if we are to decide and judge for ourselves. The hidden life is full of temptations, perplexities and dangers, and it is not safe to en-

counter them alone.   The thing is to make a good
choice in seeking a director.   Ask God to help you
in so important a matter, and be sure He will not
fail you.   Earthly motives and likings are almost
sure to mislead you, but God often makes the way
plain by an indescribable drawing which leads us to
put full confidence in some one of His servants; he
seems to have a special gift for calming the soul,
clearing away its doubts and scruples, and setting
us at rest—his words stir us greatly, and stimulate
our ardour in holy things, and a general sense of
reverence, love and submission fills our hearts in his
presence.   These are indications that we have found
a suitable director.   Probably we shall be confirmed
by experience in this conviction ; were it to prove
otherwise, God would make it plain.   Having found
a good director, it is next no small matter to make
a right use of him.   The more interior your life,
the easier this will be.   General rules are not of
much use, but so much I would say, Let your intercourse concern spiritual things only, as far as may
be—and let mutual respect and seriousness prevail,
ever remembering that God is the witness of
all your interviews.   Conceal nothing from your
director, under any pretext, even if you should feel
doubtful or suspicious of him.   Satan is always try-

ing to undermine your confidence in your spiritual guide, as his best means of keeping you from God. What you shrink most from telling is generally that which it is most necessary to tell. Obey simply and heartily, without arguing and discussing your director's opinions. Above all, fix your heart on God, see Him in all things, do not cling in an earthly spirit to your director, and if you should be deprived of one to whom you are attached, be content that God Who gave him should take him away. If He were to deprive you of all human aid, He would assuredly Himself be your Guide, and supply all your need.

God's Abiding Care for us

ST. PAUL says that "all things work together for good to them that love God;" and this is in truth the very foundation of the whole spiritual life. Mark how the Apostle says "all things," without any exception. Every event, whether it involves pleasure or pain ; all that concerns health, welfare, or repute ; all the varying conditions of our outer life, as those which affect the inner life of the soul,—privation, dryness, weariness, temptation, failings,—each and all "work together for good." But the "good" is not of this world. Under the former covenant God rewarded His faithful servants with temporal blessings ; under the new covenant He has told them to expect sorrow, the cross and persecution, and to look for no reward, save one that is supernatural. It is then to our spiritual good that all these things tend, and moreover that good is measured by our Father's judgment, not ours, nor does He see as we see. "His ways are not as our ways, or His thoughts as our thoughts."

We are apt to deceive ourselves strangely, and to imagine the very reverse of what is our real good —and therefore it behoves us to rest content in the certainty that whatever our Heavenly Father orders, whether as concerns our natural or spiritual life, is our true good, however little we may be able to understand what He does, or to foresee whither He is leading us.

But there is a condition which must not be forgotten. All things work together for good only for "those that love God ;" that is for such as have surrendered their will wholly to God, and who seek His pleasure and glory in all they do, ready to give all they have and are to Him, desiring to lose themselves in God, that they may indeed be found in Him. "He that loveth his life shall lose it, and he that hateth his life for My Sake in this world shall keep it unto life eternal."[1] Whosoever attains such love as this may rest assured that whatever comes will work for his exceeding gain ; he may not see it at the time, sight often hinders faith in such matters, but he will see it, and marvel that he could ever have thought that to be an evil which was working his salvation. "What I do thou knowest not now, but thou shalt know hereafter."

[1] John xii. 25 ; Matt. x. 39.

God Only is Holy, He Alone knows how to lead His children in the paths of holiness. He knows every aspect of your soul, every thought of your heart, every secret of your character, its difficulties and hindrances; He knows how to mould you to His Will and lead you onwards to perfect sanctification ; He knows exactly how each event, each trial, each temptation, will tell upon you, and He disposes all things accordingly. His love is everlasting; "We love Him because He first loved us." Nothing save your want of perfect trust and confidence can prevent all things from forwarding your real good, and leading you onwards to the fulness of your promised blessedness.

The consequences of this belief, if fully grasped, will influence your whole life. You will seek to give yourself up to God more and more unreservedly, asking nothing, wishing nothing, refusing nothing but what He wills; not seeking to bring things about for yourself, taking all He sends joyfully, and believing the "one step" set before you to be enough for you. You will be satisfied that even though there are clouds around, and your way seems dark, He is directing all, and that what seems a hindrance will prove a blessing since He wills it. Even with respect to spiritual trials you will feel this, and when you are dull and lifeless in prayer, disturbed by fears or temptations, you will know that He is working for your good. His Grace is often most powerful when we are least able to realize its actual presence; "When I am weak then am I strong." All your strength is in God, in simple faith, in abstaining from all self-seeking, all self-reliance. Hope against hope, and say "I know in Whom I have trusted." Another consequence of this entire trust in God is that you will be ready for any sacrifice, above all the sacrifice of your own opinion. You must be prepared to put aside all the wilfulness of your own reason and instinct, to accept mortifications and humiliations which are hard to bear, to bear the purging of your heart and soul as by fire. All this is hard to nature, but true love of God will enable you to bear it. If the Apostle's words are true, and *all things* work together for your good, dare you pick out this or that trial as the exception, and shrink from it? Let St. Paul again supply you with a profession of faith. " I reckon that the sufferings of this present time are not worthy to be compared with the glory which shall be revealed in us. . . . In all these things we are more than conquerors through Him that loved us."

The Soul's True Value

WHILE, on the one hand, religion humbles us, teaching as it does, that we are less than nothing, conceived in sin, predisposed to evil, incapable of any supernatural good, on the other hand, it sets before us a far higher estimate of our soul's worth than any we could imagine for ourselves, when it makes known how God has wrought our salvation, and the great things He has in store for us. The soul is endowed with a power of knowing and loving God; with a gift of intelligence capable of rising above all created beings to Him Who Alone is uncreate; a gift of will to love Him, an incapacity to be satisfied with anything short of His Infinite perfection. Try to analyse your own ideas of happiness, you will find that ultimately it must rest in God. Even heathen philosophers of old worked out this truth in a more or less definite shape; and in proportion to the clearness of their perceptions, they estimated the dignity of man. Nor do we stop here, the soul is created with a view to the eternal possession of God; it is not merely immortal, it is destined to be united to Him, the Source of Immortality, to share His everlasting blessedness. Immortality, were it not "satisfied with His plenteousness," would be rather a curse than a blessing. But there is a condition attached to this eternal possession of God: it is to be won by a right use of free-will during the short probation of this life, God Himself helping us with His Grace to make that right use of His gifts. It consists in loving and seeking Him, in obeying His laws, which indeed "are not grievous," and which tend to earthly peace and happiness as well as to Heavenly Rest. Considered thus, man is a glorious being! but take the opposite side, and what a miserable, contemptible thing he is, when he refuses to seek God, and prefers the empty cisterns of this world to the "well of life" springing up to salvation. "Be astonished, O ye heavens at this, and be horribly afraid, be ye very desolate, saith the Lord; for My people have committed two evils; they have forsaken Me the fountain of living waters, and hewed them out cisterns, broken cisterns, that can hold no water."[1] In theory we should scarce deem it possible that men

[1] Jer. ii. 12, 13.

should forget, despise, outrage Him Who made
them, and sustains them, and that because He would
have them share His everlasting bliss, and therefore
requires of them to abstain for a little while from
the pleasures of sin.   Yet in practice we all are
ready to fix our eyes longingly on the land of our
exile, rather than on our true home ; we over estimate this world's treasures, as much as we slight
those held out to us ; we shrink from death as
though it were the end, not the beginning of our
true life.

But the height of our dignity is the price set on
man by God in sending His Word, Co-Equal and
Co-Eternal with the Father, to take upon Him the
form of man, to dwell with him, to teach him, to die
for him.   What our Dear Lord did for mankind generally, He did for each separate individual human
being throughout all ages ; each soul that exists
has cost His Life Blood, His Great Mysterious Sacrifice.   It is past man's understanding, we can but
take it on trust ; we cannot fathom the mighty
truth, we only KNOW it.   But it makes us realise
that a Soul is a very precious thing, and that if
Jesus thought it worth so infinite a price, we can
scarcely estimate it too highly, or shrink from proving our belief in its value, by co-operating with Him

for its salvation. Look at the Cross, if you would learn the true value of a soul, your own soul, the soul of each human being for whom you can do somewhat; measure and weigh your life, your sufferings, your joys, your hopes, by that standard; see wherein you are wanting, towards your own soul, or your brethren's, and remember that "if our heart condemn us, God is greater than our heart, and knoweth all things."

Purity of Intention

OUR Lord has said, " If thine eye be single, thy whole body shall be full of light." Now intention is the eye of the soul, its motive power and guiding force; and if this eye be single, that is if your intention be pure, with God for its undivided aim, free from self-interest, then your actions will be holy and full of God's own Light. Singleness of intention implies purity and straightforwardness. Your intention is straightforward when you act in perfect good faith, not seeking to deceive yourself, but honestly following after truth. This sounds plain enough, but nevertheless it is not very common among men—prejudice, error, passion, vice, many less obvious infirmities interfere, and deceive the conscience; nothing save constant watchfulness against your great enemy, self-love, will be any security on this score. A pure intention must have no object but God, it must be free from the snares of self; and in fact such purity of intention is the very essential of all holiness. While we love God for our own sake, and seek His favours for our own interest; in short, while self is the point to which all our thoughts tend, we cannot be said to have that purity of intention which is most acceptable in God's Sight. Of course a single intention implies oneness of aim, and this sanctifies even the smallest actions; the most trifling thing done solely to please God is more precious in His Sight than all possible austerities and mighty deeds, prompted by vain-glory or self-love ; and that because He looks at the motive which prompts the deed, rather than at its result. It is the same among men ; do you not value any service rendered to you in proportion to the affection which prompts it, rather than to the thing itself? Only we are unable really to read the mysteries of one another's hearts, whereas God sees every impulse and desire we can form. We all crave for attention, and often value small acts of consideration very highly, because they are signs of love—the wish to please is more acceptable to most of us than all else.

Such purity of intention can only be attained by giving yourself up wholly to God, asking Him to direct and guide, not only your outer life, but every thought and wish of your heart. Ask Him to kindle in you hopes and affections worthy of Himself; ask Him to purge out the hidden leaven of self. You may have much to suffer ere the prayer be fully granted, but the end will be blessed. But in this, as in all else that concerns the spiritual life, do not be in a hurry. Be content to go on quietly. When you discover somewhat in yourself which is earthly and imperfect, be patient while you strive to cast it out. Your perceptions will grow,—at first God will shew you very obvious stumbling-blocks, be diligent in clearing these away, and do not aim at heights to which you are not yet equal. Leave all to God, and while you earnestly desire that He would purify your intention, and seek to work with Him to that end, be satisfied with the gradual progress He sets before you; bridle your imagination, and remember that He often works in ways unseen by us.

You may perhaps ask whether it is not necessary always to direct the intention aright? But when you have once given yourself wholly to God, such a formal act need not be constantly renewed—your general deliberate intention to please God and do His Will suffices—and it is better not to fix your attention on yourself by continually renewing such acts. If you perceive that you are in any way recalling the wholesale offering you once made of

yourself to God, there is nothing to be done but
once more to restore Him that which is His, and
renew your self-renunciation. It is well to make
such an act of general intention every morning ; it
includes all other acts, and is of all the most profitable to your inner life. The intention to accept
God's Will in all things implies all else, such as
doing His good pleasure, and avoiding what is displeasing to Him, and it has the special advantage
of not helping to concentrate our thoughts in any
way upon ourselves. As you advance in the interior
life, be sure that self will dwindle in importance,
and God will become all in all, and this it is which
the "single eye" attains.

Mary and Martha

WE learn a weighty lesson concerning the interior life from the history of these sisters;
Martha being the type of an active life, seeking to
set forth its love of God by voluntary toil and effort;
Mary the type of a contemplative life which seeks
to abide in absolute stillness, waiting to receive an
impulse from God only. Both sisters were glad to
welcome the Lord under their roof, both loved
Him, both sought to prove their love, but in very
different ways. Martha's aim was to supply her
Lord's temporal wants, and she was eager, careful,
anxious in her labour, while Mary gave no outer
token of her love, content to sit at Jesus' Feet and
drink in His life-giving words; the one all exterior
life and action; the other all interior silence and
rest. One seeks to give, the other to receive; one
eagerly offers all she has, the other silently gives
herself. Martha in her activity thought that Mary
was neglecting their Lord; but in answer to her

appeal, Jesus told her that Mary had chosen "the better part." This answer will help us not a little to check the restlessness and over-activity which are besetting hindrances to the spiritual life. Doubtless it was fitting that the sisters should provide for their Master's wants, but Martha was eager, busy, troubled ; moreover, she thought more highly of her own doings than of her sister's. Therefore the Lord rebuked her, shewing her that however good external works may be, essential of course in a certain measure, still they are but for this world ; whereas the hidden life which begins on earth, continues to rise perpetually upwards, until it finds its perfection in Heaven. It was the same when on the occasion of Lazarus' death Jesus went to the sisters—Martha went eagerly to meet Him ; Mary waited till the Master was come and called for her ; the one acted on her own impulses, the other received all impulses from Christ. Now, from all this we may gather, that good works, however valuable, are of less importance than prayer and contemplation ; and that it is not well to let ourselves be so absorbed in active works of charity, as to hinder or stifle the inner life. Zeal and charity are admirable things, but zeal requires to be well regulated, and charity must begin at

home. Then, too, where there is no question as to
the duty of external works; where God indeed
requires them of us, we should strive to fulfil them
without losing the spirit of interior calmness, doing
all with recollection and in union with God. This
is by no means easy, and therefore many spiritual
guides advise beginners to study prayer and meditation rather than active good works, until the
habit of recollection is so formed that they can
give themselves freely to external things without
losing inward rest. At all times that restless
activity, even in the inner life, which comes from
self-love is an evil to be steadily repressed. Mary
sat still at Jesus' Feet; she did not talk, or question
Him, she only gathered up each precious word as
it fell; and so the devout soul must not squander
its warmth and freshness in many words or feelings,
but rather wait silently for God's Grace to work
within. Restless activity multiplies devotions and
practices, it is given to change, it is never satisfied;
but a tranquil spirit is concentrated on God, and
whether in prayer or other duties it seeks only to
fulfil His Will in the actual moment that passes,
leaving all past and future to Him, losing itself in
the thought of God, its one object and sole end.
Thus you will learn how to combine the duties of

Mary and Martha so that neither should suffer loss. You will not neglect any claim, even such as courtesy puts forward, but every duty will be sanctified by your inseparable union with God, and your continual dependence upon His Grace. You will readily do whatever you can for your neighbour, according as God points out the way,—not officiously or in self-seeking zeal ; even in the holiest duties you will prefer to go where God calls you, rather than where your own fancy or choice may lead. You will accept whatever may be your actual condition, because it is that appointed by Him. How happy and peaceful, how useful to man, how acceptable to God we should be, if we could always set aside our love of self-guidance, and serve Him thus!

"Alway with God"

*" So foolish was I, and ignorant, even as it were a beast before Thee ;
nevertheless I am alway by Thee."*—PSA. lxxiii. 21.

THE two clauses are remarkable—to be " as a beast before God," and yet " alway by Him." Our idea of a holy life and close intercourse with God was something other than this ! and yet it is His Holy Spirit which speaks.   What is it to be as a beast of burden ? Is it not to give all one's strength and power, without any choice or limit, to a master's service ; to bear what he lays on one, go whither he wills, as he wills, by the road he appoints, at the pace he chooses, halting for food and rest solely when it pleases him ?   And is not this a fitting attitude for the soul with respect to God ? The soul that would be " alway with Him," must depend on Him Alone for everything ;—it must renounce all self-chosen ways and wills, accepting whatever God may appoint, above all in what concerns the inner life.   And this dependence can only

be attained by complete self-abnegation, abnegation
of the intellectual faculties as well as in other things,
content to endure dryness in prayer and Holy
Communion, and to be deprived of all sensible
sweetness in religious exercises. In your intercourse with your neighbours, you must not be
studied or affected; nor dwell upon the faults of
others; you must speak your own mind honestly,
careless as to whether you are admired or despised, and refrain from thinking about it afterwards.
When alone, you must strive after a free spirit, not
allowing yourself to wander at the will of your
imagination among things past or future; you must
repress curiosity, not meddle with other people's
affairs, and try to deal with what concerns your
own as in the world, not of it. Your heart must be
free from all attachments save what God chooses—
you must ask and fear nothing, claim nothing as
your own. Those who have once tasted the sweetness of union with God, do not find it very hard to
be detached from earthly things, but it is not so
easy to sit loose even to spiritual gifts;—to be
without that interior peace, that consciousness of
God's Presence which seemed once our own for
ever. Nor is it easy to submit to ridicule, contempt,
harsh judgments, without self-defence. "In time

of temptation," our Lord says, many such "fall away."[1]   But a generous soul, which relies solely on God, will bear all such trials, as gold cast into the furnace, and come forth purified.   Yes, it is this voluntary subjection that leads to being "alway with God," and sometimes He is in truth nearest when the soul fancies Him afar off.   Even our Dear Lord cried out from the Cross, " My God, why hast Thou forsaken Me?" and yet in truth the Father had not forsaken Him, through He permitted the fiercest tempest of His Wrath to pass over the Son of Man. For a little while He may hide His Face, but soon the veil will be withdrawn for ever—and the days of mourning shall be ended for the faithful souls which have "waited for the Loving-kindness of the Lord."

[1] Luke viii. 13.

Death

THE thought of death is fearful to those who are living in sin; they cannot avert the reality, but at least they strive to banish the thought. It is fearful too, to such as serve God from self-interest only, whose eyes are fixed on their own unworthy selves, and who dwell more on God's Justice than His Mercy. Generally speaking, the thought of death must be painful to those who are not really detached from the things of this world, who have not striven to die to self and its interests.

But on the other hand, it is a welcome thought to those hidden souls who have heartily given themselves to God, and trusting all in His Hands, seek nothing save His Love: as to the former death is the end, so to the latter it is as the beginning of happiness. Want of confidence in God makes the hour of death to be a terror, but those who have put all their trust in Him know no limit to that which they look for at His Hands. To them death is the

blessed moment which will set them free for ever
from all temptation to sin, from all possibility of
displeasing God. Love has hitherto been their
life, and now that life is to become unchanging, everlasting; there is no question in such minds as to
the future. God is God—they love Him; their sins
are manifold, but they firmly reject them all, and
cast themselves freely upon His Infinite Mercy.
They dwell upon the thought that Jesus Christ is
their Judge, and say within themselves, "How can
I dread Him Who has dealt so lovingly with me,
Who has guided me hitherto, Who has drawn me
to Himself with such boundless Love, Whose Love
will not leave me while the last feeble breath
struggles within me?" How can such an one cling
to life? How can such an one fear death, which is
the passage to His Presence Who is Life Itself, the
Sole Good for which he has panted? He has ever
borne about with him one lowly, chastening fear;
the fear that anything should loosen his firm hold
upon God. Through life, temptations are ever at
hand, what humble soul does say that he *cannot*
fall? But death puts an end to this fear—"Thou
knowest, Lord, the secrets of our hearts; shut not
Thy merciful ears to our prayer, but spare us, O
Lord most holy, O God most Mighty; O holy and

Merciful Saviour, Thou most worthy Judge Eternal, suffer us not at our last hour, for any pains of death, to fall from Thee." "Thanks be to God, Which giveth us the Victory through our Lord Jesus Christ."

Be sure that you will look to death, according to your manner of life. If a pure heart and mortified spirit have broken down the earthly barrier between you and God ; if trial and sacrifice have brought you into a close realisation of the Cross, to union with God, you cannot fear death ; you will see it from His Side only, and in no way from your own, all that is fearful is lost when merged in His Holy Will. Death is wholly loveable and peaceful seen in the Light of His Love. " Perfect love casteth out fear ;" "O death, where is thy sting ? O grave, where is thy victory ? "

These are weighty truths, only to be realised as we draw nearer God ; but those who cannot as yet fully grasp them, may believe that they are truths by the light of faith, and by the witness of countless holy souls who have proved them, and " know in Whom they have believed."

Having said this, it may seem strange to add that those who are living a very interior life will generally dwell but little on the thought of death. God fills

their heart, and absorbs it, and as the thought of
death arises chiefly from the power it has over man's
imagination, those whose imagination is most repressed by their growing spirituality will gradually
lose the fear of death, which will come before them
more from a heavenly than an earthly point of view.
And assuredly God would not have a soul which
clings to Him scared at the thought of the last
narrow passage to be crossed in reaching Him. But
no set words or thoughts will enable us to meet
death trustfully. Such trust is God's Gift, and the
more we can detach ourselves from all save Himself, the more "freely He will give us" this, as all
other blessings. Once attain to losing self in God,
and death will indeed have no sting. We are wont
to exhort one class of Christians to meditate upon
death, its uncertainty, its terrors, in order that they
may see how they live. But those who have attained
to the interior life, need not dwell on this side of
the question, God calls them rather to a perpetual
mystical death, death to self, in will, in thought,
in deed; so that when the actual moment of material
death arrives, it is but the final passage to eternal
joy for them. Let your constant prayer be as regards death, " When Thou wilt, as Thou wilt, and
where Thou wilt," and all will in truth be well for you.

Eternity

WE tremble at the thought of eternity, and well we may; but if the fear was turned to good account, we should soon learn to rejoice in trembling. To those who yield unrestrainedly to their passions, the thought of eternity must needs be terrible. Yet they too might well pause and think whether they do well to sacrifice an eternal future to the moment of time now passing. Those too who cling tightly to the joys and hopes of this life may tremble to feel that what they cherish most is gliding from beneath their grasp, and eternity alone remains. But then arises the question, If all this is so soon to pass away, why should I cleave so closely to it? Why not seek that which endureth for ever rather than that which is but as foam upon the sea, as lightning in the midnight sky? Again, some timid souls shrink from the thought of their possible condemnation, and loss of that blessed eternity promised to the faithful. But let such remember that God loves them better than they love themselves; that He desires their salvation more earnestly than they desire it; that He has given them unfailing means of salvation if they will but use such means. What more need they save faith and trust? Their overweening fearfulness comes of self,—of measuring God by their own poor standard, rather than themselves by His boundless greatness. They have not looked chiefly at His Glory, His Will, His Love, but at themselves. Let them look higher, and fear will yield to love; peace will come to their souls, and eternity will cease to dismay them.

It must do more;—it must become a source of abiding rest and joy. Hear St. Paul telling us that "our light affliction, which is but for a moment, worketh for us a far more exceeding and eternal weight of glory."[1] Will not this thought carry you over many waves of this troublesome life, through many heartaches, and wearinesses, and sorrows? A Saint of old was wont to ask of any subject presented to him, "How does it affect eternal life?" Will it hinder or help my eternal happiness? Such a test would solve most of our vexed questions. Let it be the rule of your life, try all things by it, make it your abiding thought.

"Let us go forth therefore unto Him without the camp, bearing His reproach: for here have we no abiding city, but we seek one to come."

[1] 2 Cor. iv. 17.

September, 1870.

𝔑𝔢𝔴 𝔚𝔬𝔯𝔨𝔰

IN COURSE OF PUBLICATION

BY

Messrs. RIVINGTON,

WATERLOO PLACE, LONDON;

HIGH STREET, OXFORD ; TRINITY STREET, CAMBRIDGE.

Elements of Religion: Lectures deli-
vered at St. James', Piccadilly, in Lent, 1870.
  By **Henry Parry Liddon**, D.C.L., Canon of St. Paul's, and
Ireland Professor of Exegesis in the University of Oxford.
Crown 8vo. (*In Preparation.*)

A Plain Account of the English Bible,
from the Earliest Times of its Translation to the Present Day.
  By **John Henry Blunt**, M.A., F.S.A., Vicar of Kennington,
Oxford ; Author of "The History of the Reformation of the
Church of England;" Editor of "The Annotated Book of
Common Prayer," &c.
Crown 8vo. 3*s.* 6*d.*

𝔏𝔬𝔫𝔡𝔬𝔫, 𝔒𝔵𝔣𝔬𝔯𝔡, 𝔞𝔫𝔡 𝔠𝔞𝔪𝔟𝔯𝔦𝔡𝔤𝔢

A

The Origin and Development of Religious Belief.

By **8. Baring-Gould**, M.A., Author of "Curious Myths of the Middle Ages."

Part I. Heathenism and Mosaism. 8vo. 15s.
Part II. Christianity. (*In the Press.*)

The Pope and the Council.

By **Janus**. Authorized Translation from the German.
Third Edition, revised. Crown 8vo. 7s. 6d.

The Ammergau Passion Play.

Reprinted, by permission, from the *Times*. With some Introductory Remarks on the Origin and Development of Miracle Plays, and some Practical Hints for the use of Intending Visitors.

By the Rev. **Malcolm MacColl**, M.A., Chaplain to the Right Hon. Lord Napier, K.T.

Second Edition. Crown 8vo. 2s. 6d.

Letters from Rome on the Council.

By **Quirinus**. Reprinted from the *Allgemeine Zeitung*. Authorized Translation.

The First Series contains Preliminary History of the Council and Letters I. to XV. Crown 8vo. 3s. 6d.

The Second Series contains Letters XVI. to XXXIV. Crown 8vo. 3s. 6d.

Volume I. will be completed in the Third Series, now in the Press.

The Church of God and the Bishops:

An Essay suggested by the Convocation of the Vatican Council.
By **Henry St. A. Von Liaño**. Authorized Translation.
Crown 8vo. 4s. 6d.

Our Lord's Passion;

being the Seventh Volume of a DEVOTIONAL COMMENTARY ON THE GOSPEL NARRATIVE (v. page 28).

By the Rev. Isaac Williams, B.D., late Fellow of Trinity College, Oxford.

New Edition. Crown 8vo. 5s.

The First Book of Common Prayer

of Edward VI. and the Ordinal of 1549; together with the Order of the Communion, 1548.

Reprinted entire, and Edited by the Rev. Henry Baskerville Walton, M.A., late Fellow and Tutor of Merton College. With Introduction by the Rev. Peter Goldsmith Medd, M.A., Senior Fellow and Tutor of University College, Oxford.

Small 8vo. 6s.

A Manual for the Sick; with other

Devotions.

By Lancelot Andrewes, D.D., sometime Lord Bishop of Winchester.

Edited with a Preface by Henry Parry Liddon, D.C.L., Canon of St. Paul's.

Second Edition. Large type. With Portrait. 24mo. 2s. 6d.

The Pursuit of Holiness:

a Sequel to "Thoughts on Personal Religion," intended to carry the Reader somewhat farther onward in the Spiritual Life.

By Edward Meyrick Goulburn, D.D., Dean of Norwich.

Second Edition. Small 8vo. 5s.

Apostolical Succession in the Church

of England.

By the Rev. Arthur W. Haddan, B.D., Rector of Barton-on-the-Heath, and late Fellow of Trinity College, Oxford.

8vo. 12s.

The Priest to the Altar ; or, Aids to

the Devout Celebration of Holy Communion ; chiefly after the
Ancient Use of Sarum.

Second Edition. Enlarged, Revised, and Re-arranged with
the Secretæ, Post-Communion, &c., appended to the Collects,
Epistles, and Gospels, throughout the Year.

8vo. 7s. 6d.

Walter Kerr Hamilton : Bishop of

Salisbury. A Sketch, Reprinted, with Additions and Corrections, from "The Guardian."

By **Henry Parry Liddon**, D.C.L., Canon of St. Paul's.

Second Edition. 8vo, limp cloth, 2s. 6d.

Or, bound with the Sermon "Life in Death," 3s. 6d.

Newman's (J.H.) Parochial and Plain

Sermons.

Edited by the Rev. **W. J. Copeland**, Rector of Farnham,
Essex. From the Text of the last Editions published by
Messrs. Rivington.

In 8 Vols. Crown 8vo. 5s. each.

Newman's (J.H.) Sermons bearing upon

Subjects of the Day.

Edited by the Rev. **W. J. Copeland**, Rector of Farnham,
Essex. From the Text of the last Edition published by Messrs.
Rivington. With Index of Dates of all the Sermons.

Printed uniformly with the "Parochial and Plain Sermons."

In One Volume. Crown 8vo. 5s.

Brighstone Sermons.

By **George Moberly**, D.C.L., Bishop of Salisbury.

Second Edition. Crown 8vo. 7s. 6d.

The Characters of the Old Testament.

In a Series of Sermons.

By the Rev. Isaac Williams, B.D., late Fellow of Trinity College, Oxford.

New Edition.   Crown 8vo.   5s.

Female Characters of Holy Scripture.

In a Series of Sermons.

By the Rev. Isaac Williams, B.D., late Fellow of Trinity College, Oxford.

New Edition.   Crown 8vo.   5s.

The Divinity of our Lord and Saviour

Jesus Christ; being the Bampton Lectures for 1866.

By Henry Parry Liddon, D.C.L., Canon of St. Paul's, and Ireland Professor of Exegesis in the University of Oxford.

Fourth Edition.   Crown 8vo.   5s.

Sermons preached before the University

of Oxford.

By Henry Parry Liddon, D.C.L., Canon of St. Paul's, and Ireland Professor of Exegesis in the University of Oxford.

Third Edition, revised.   Crown 8vo.   5s.

The Life of Madame Louise de France,

Daughter of Louis XV., also known as the Mother Térèse de S. Augustin.   By the Author of "Tales of Kirkbeck."

Crown 8vo.   6s.

John Wesley's Place in Church His-
tory Determined, with the aid of Facts and Documents
unknown to, or unnoticed by, his Biographers.
> By **R. Denny Urlin**, M.R.I.A., of the Middle Temple,
> Barrister-at-Law.
> With a New and Authentic Portrait. Small 8vo. 5*s.* 6*d.*

The Treasury of Devotion: a Manual
of Prayers for general and daily use.
> Compiled by a Priest. Edited by the Rev. **T. T. Carter**,
> M.A., Rector of Clewer, Berks.
>> 16mo, limp cloth, 2*s.*; cloth extra, 2*s.* 6*d.*
>> Bound with the Book of Common Prayer. 3*s.* 6*d.*

The Guide to Heaven: a Book of
Prayers for every Want. For the Working Classes.
> Compiled by a Priest. Edited by the Rev. **T. T. Carter**,
> M.A., Rector of Clewer, Berks.
>> Crown 8vo, limp cloth, 1*s.*; cloth extra, 1*s.* 6*d.*

A Dominican Artist: a Sketch of the
Life of the Rev. Père Besson of the Order of St. Dominic.
> By the Author of "Tales of Kirkbeck," "The Life of
> Madame Louise de France," &c.
>> Crown 8vo. 9*s.*

The Reformation of the Church of
England; its History, Principles, and Results. A.D. 1514—1547.
> By **John Henry Blunt**, M.A., Vicar of Kennington, Oxford,
> Editor of "The Annotated Book of Common Prayer,"
> Author of "Directorium Pastorale," &c., &c.
>> *Second Edition.* 8vo. 16*s.*

London, Oxford, and Cambridge

The Virgin's Lamp :

Prayers and Devout Exercises for English Sisters, chiefly composed and selected by the late Rev. J. M. Neale, D.D., Founder of St. Margaret's, East Grinstead.

Small 8vo.   3s. 6d.

Catechetical Notes and Class Questions,

Literal and Mystical; chiefly on the Earlier Books of Holy Scripture.

By the late Rev. J. M. Neale, D.D., Warden of Sackville College, East Grinstead.

Crown 8vo.   5s.

Sermons for Children ; being Thirty-

three short Readings, addressed to the Children of S. Margaret's Home, East Grinstead.

By the late Rev. J. M. Neale, D.D., Warden of Sackville College.

Second Edition.   Small 8vo.   3s. 6d.

The Witness of the Old Testament to

Christ.   The Boyle Lectures for the Year 1868.

By the Rev. Stanley Leathes, M.A., Professor of Hebrew in King's College, London, and Incumbent of St. Philip's, Regent Street.

8vo.   9s.

The Witness of St. Paul to Christ ;

being the Boyle Lectures for 1869.   With an Appendix, on the Credibility of the Acts, in Reply to the Recent Strictures of Dr. Davidson.

By the Rev. Stanley Leathes, M.A., Professor of Hebrew in King's College, London, and Incumbent of St. Philip's, Regent Street.

8vo.   10s. 6d.

Honoré de Balzac.

Edited, with English Notes and Introductory Notice, by **Henri Van Laun**, formerly French Master at Cheltenham College, and now Master of the French Language and Literature at the Edinburgh Academy. Being the first Volume of Selections from Modern French Authors.

Crown 8vo. 3*s.* 6*d.*

H. A. Taine.

Edited, with English Notes and Introductory Notice, by **Henri Van Laun**, formerly French Master at Cheltenham College, and now Master of the French Language and Literature at the Edinburgh Academy. Being the second Volume of Selections from Modern French Authors.

Crown 8vo. 3*s.* 6*d.*

The Greek Testament.

With a Critically revised Text; a Digest of Various Readings; Marginal References to Verbal and Idiomatic Usage; Prolegomena; and a Critical and Exegetical Commentary. For the use of Theological Students and Ministers.

By **Henry Alford**, D.D., Dean of Canterbury.

4 Vols. 8vo. 102*s.*

The Volumes are sold separately as follows :—

Vol. I.—The Four Gospels. *Sixth Edition.* 28*s.*
Vol. II.—Acts to II. Corinthians. *Fifth Edition.* 24*s.*
Vol. III.—Galatians to Philemon. *Fourth Edition.* 18*s.*
Vol. IV.—Hebrews to Revelation. *Fourth Edition.* 32*s.*

Dean Alford's Greek Testament.

With English Notes, intended for the Upper Forms of Schools, and for Pass-men at the Universities. Abridged by **Bradley H. Alford**, M.A., late Scholar of Trinity College, Cambridge.

Crown 8vo. 10*s.* 6*d.*

Elementary Algebra.

By **James Hamblin Smith**, M.A., Gonville and Caius College, and Lecturer at St. Peter's College, Cambridge.

Second Edition, Revised and Enlarged. Crown 8vo. 4s. 6d.

Elementary Trigonometry.

By **James Hamblin Smith**, M.A., Gonville and Caius College, and Lecturer at St. Peter's College, Cambridge.

Second Edition, Revised and Enlarged. Crown 8vo. 4s. 6d.

Elementary Statics.

By **James Hamblin Smith**, M.A., Gonville and Caius College, and Lecturer at St. Peter's College, Cambridge.

Royal 8vo. 5s.

Elementary Hydrostatics.

By **James Hamblin Smith**, M.A., Gonville and Caius College, and Lecturer at St. Peter's College, Cambridge.

Second Edition, Revised and Enlarged. Crown 8vo. 3s.

Arithmetic, Theoretical and Practical.

By **W. H. Girdlestone**, M.A., of Christ's College, Cambridge, Principal of the Theological College, Gloucester.

Second Edition, Revised and Enlarged. Crown 8vo. 6s. 6d.

Also an Edition for Schools. Small 8vo. 3s. 6d.

Classical Examination Papers.

Edited, with Notes and References. By **P. J. F. Gantillon**,
M.A., sometime Scholar of St. John's College, Cambridge,
Classical Master in Cheltenham College.

Crown 8vo. 7s. 6d.

Materials and Models for Greek and

Latin Prose Composition. Selected and arranged by **J. Y.
Sargent**, M.A., Tutor, late Fellow of Magdalen College,
Oxford ; and **T. F. Dallin**, M.A., Fellow and Tutor of Queen's
College, Oxford.

Crown 8vo. (*In the Press.*)

The Story of the Gospels.

In a single Narrative, combined from the Four Evangelists,
showing in a new translation their unity. To which is added a
like continuous Narrative in the Original Greek.

By the Rev. **William Pound**, M.A., late Fellow of St. John's
College, Cambridge, Principal of Appuldurcombe School, Isle
of Wight.

In 2 Vols. 8vo. 36s.

The Lyrics of Horace.

Done into English Rhyme. By **Thomas Charles Baring**, M.A.,
late Fellow of Brasenose College, Oxford.

Small 4to. 7s.

A Plain and Short History of England

for Children : in Letters from a Father to his Son. With a
Set of Questions at the end of each Letter.

By **George Davys**, D.D., late Bishop of Peterborough.
New Edition, with Twelve coloured Illustrations.

Square Crown 8vo. 3s. 6d.

A Cheap Edition for Schools, with portrait of Edward VI.

18mo. 1s. 6d.

Memoir of the Right Rev. John

Strachan, D.D., LL.D., First Bishop of Toronto.
By A. N. Bethune, D.D., D.C.L., his Successor in the See.
8vo. 10s.

A Course of Lectures delivered to Can-

didates for Holy Orders, comprising a Summary of the whole
System of Theology. To which is prefixed an Inaugural
Address.
By John Randolph, D.D. (sometime Bishop of London).
Vol. I. Natural and Revealed.
Vol. II. Historical.
Vol. III. Doctrinal.
3 Vols. 8vo. 7s. 6d. each.

History of the College of St. John the

Evangelist, Cambridge.
By Thomas Baker, B.D., Ejected Fellow.
Edited for the Syndics of the University Press, by John
E. B. Mayor, M.A., Fellow of St. John's College.
2 Vols. 8vo. 24s.

The Annotated Book of Common

Prayer; being an Historical, Ritual, and Theological Com-
mentary on the Devotional System of the Church of England.
Edited by John Henry Blunt, M.A.
Fourth Edition. Imperial 8vo. 36s.

London, Oxford, and Cambridge

The Prayer Book Interleaved;

with Historical Illustrations and Explanatory Notes arranged parallel to the Text, by the Rev. **W. M. Campion**, D.D., Fellow and Tutor of Queens' College and Rector of St. Botolph's, and the Rev. **W. J. Beamont**, M.A., late Fellow of Trinity College, Cambridge. With a Preface by the **Lord Bishop of Ely.**

Fifth Edition. Small 8vo. 7s. 6d.

Flowers and Festivals; or, Directions

for the Floral Decorations of Churches. With coloured Illustrations.

By **W. A. Barrett**, of S. Paul's Cathedral, late Clerk of Magdalen College, and Commoner of S. Mary Hall, Oxford.

Square Crown 8vo. 5s.

Light in the Heart; or, Short Medita-

tions on Subjects which concern the Soul. Translated from the French.

Edited by the Rev. **W. J. Butler**, M.A., Vicar of Wantage.

18mo. 1s. 6d.

Consoling Thoughts in Sickness.

Edited by **Henry Bailey**, B.D., Warden of St. Augustine's College, Canterbury.

Large type. *Fine Edition.* Small 8vo. 2s. 6d.

Also a Cheap Edition, 1s. 6d. ; or in Paper Cover, 1s.

Sickness; its Trials and Blessings.

Fine Edition, on toned paper. Small 8vo. 3s. 6d.

Also a Cheap Edition, 1s. 6d., or in Paper Cover, 1s.

Help and Comfort for the Sick Poor.

By the Author of "Sickness ; its Trials and Blessings."

New Edition. Small 8vo. 1s.

Hymns and Poems for the Sick and

Suffering ; in connexion with the Service for the Visitation of the Sick. Selected from various Authors.

Edited by **T. V. Fosbery,** M.A., Vicar of St. Giles's, Reading.

New Edition. Small 8vo. 3s. 6d.

The Dogmatic Faith: an Inquiry

into the Relation subsisting between Revelation and Dogma. Being the Bampton Lectures for 1867.

By **Edward Garbett,** M.A., Incumbent of Christ Church, Surbiton.

Second Edition. Crown 8vo. 5s.

Sketches of the Rites and Customs of

the Greco-Russian Church.

By **H. C. Romanoff.** With an Introductory Notice by the Author of "The Heir of Redclyffe."

Second Edition. Crown 8vo. 7s. 6d.

Household Theology: a Handbook of

Religious Information respecting the Holy Bible, the Prayer Book, the Church, the Ministry, Divine Worship, the Creeds, &c. &c.

By **John Henry Blunt,** M.A.

Third Edition. Small 8vo. 3s. 6d.

Curious Myths of the Middle Ages.

By **S. Baring-Gould**, M.A., Author of "Post-Mediæval
Preachers," &c.   With Illustrations.
New Edition.   Complete in one Volume.
Crown 8vo.   6*s.*

Soimême : a Story of a Wilful Life.

Small 8vo.   3*s.* 6*d.*

The Happiness of the Blessed con-

sidered as to the Particulars of their State : their Recognition
of each other in that State : and its Differences of Degrees.
To which are added Musings on the Church and Her Services.
By **Richard Mant**, D.D., sometime Lord Bishop of Down
and Connor.
New Edition.   Small 8vo.   3*s.* 6*d.*

Anglo-Saxon Witness on Four Alleged

Requisites for Holy Communion—Fasting, Water, Altar
Lights, and Incense.
By the Rev. **J. Baron**, M.A., Rector of Upton Scudamore,
Wilts.
8vo.   5*s.*

Miscellaneous Poems.

By **Henry Francis Lyte**, M.A.
New Edition.   Small 8vo.   5*s.*

The History of Tonbridge School, from

its Foundation in 1553 to the present Date.
By **Septimus Rivington**, B.A., Trinity College, Oxford.
With Illustrations.   Small 4to.   14*s.*

London, Oxford, and Cambridge

The Holy Bible.

With Notes and Introductions.
By **Chr. Wordsworth**, D.D., Bishop of Lincoln.
Imperial 8vo.

	Part	£	s.	d.
Vol. I. 38s.	I. Genesis and Exodus. *Second Edit.*	1	1	0
	II. Leviticus, Numbers, Deuteronomy. *Second Edition*	0	18	0
Vol. II. 21s.	III. Joshua, Judges, Ruth. *Second Edit.*	0	12	0
	IV. The Books of Samuel. *Second Edit.*	0	10	0
Vol. III. 21s.	V. The Books of Kings, Chronicles, Ezra, Nehemiah, Esther. *Second Edition*	1	1	0
Vol. IV. 34s.	VI. The Book of Job. *Second Edition*	0	9	0
	VII. The Book of Psalms. *Second Edit.*	0	15	0
	VIII. Proverbs, Ecclesiastes, Song of Solomon	0	12	0
Vol. V. 32s.6d	IX. Isaiah	0	12	6
	X. Jeremiah, Lamentations, and Ezekiel	1	1	0
Vol. VI.	XI. Daniel. (*In Preparation.*)			
	XII. The Minor Prophets . . .	0	12	0

Manual of Family Devotions, arranged

from the Book of Common Prayer.
By the Hon. **Augustus Duncombe**, D.D., Dean of York.
Printed in red and black.
Small 8vo. 3s. 6d.

London, Oxford, and Cambridge

Perranzabuloe, the Lost Church Found;

or, The Church of England not a New Church, but Ancient, Apostolical, and Independent, and a Protesting Church Nine Hundred Years before the Reformation.

By the Rev. C. T. Collins Trelawny, M.A., formerly Rector of Timsbury, Somerset, and late Fellow of Balliol College, Oxford.

New Edition.   Crown 8vo.   With Illustrations.   3s. 6d.

Annals of the Bodleian Library, Oxford,

from its Foundation to A.D. 1867; containing an Account of the various collections of printed books and MSS. there preserved; with a brief Preliminary Sketch of the earlier Library of the University.

By W. D. Macray, M.A., Assistant in the Library, Chaplain of Magdalen and New Colleges.

8vo.   12s.

Catechesis; or, Christian Instruction

preparatory to Confirmation and First Communion.

By Charles Wordsworth, D.C.L., Bishop of St. Andrew's.

New Edition.   Small 8vo.   2s.

Warnings of the Holy Week, &c.;

being a Course of Parochial Lectures for the Week before Easter and the Easter Festivals.

By the Rev. W. Adams, M.A., late Vicar of St. Peter's-in-the-East, Oxford, and Fellow of Merton College.

Sixth Edition.   Small 8vo.   4s. 6d.

Petronilla; and other Poems.

By Frederick George Lee, D.C.L.

Second Edition.   Small 8vo.   3s. 6d.

Consolatio ; or, Comfort for the
Afflicted.
Edited by the Rev. **C. E. Kennaway**. With a Preface by
Samuel Wilberforce, D.D., Lord Bishop of Winchester.
New Edition. Small 8vo. 3s. 6d.

Plain Scriptural Thoughts on Holy
Baptism.
By the Rev. **John Wallas**, M.A., Perpetual Curate of
Crosscrake, Westmoreland.
Crown 8vo. 6s.

A Manual of Plain Devotions, adapted
for Private and for Family Use.
By the Rev. **John Wallas**, M.A., Perpetual Curate of
Crosscrake, Westmoreland.
Second Edition. Small 8vo. 2s.

The Hillford Confirmation : a Tale.
By **M. C. Phillpotts**.
18mo. 1s.

The Greek Testament.
With Notes and Introductions.
By **Chr. Wordsworth**, D.D., Bishop of Lincoln
2 Vols. Impl. 8vo. 4l.
The Parts may be had separately, as follows :—
The Gospels, *7th Edition*, 21s.
The Acts, *5th Edition*, 10s. 6d.
St. Paul's Epistles, *5th Edition*, 31s. 6d.
General Epistles, Revelation, and Indexes, *3rd Edition*, 21s.

Occasional Sermons.

By **Henry Parry Liddon**, D.C.L., Canon of St. Paul's.
Crown 8vo. (*In Preparation.*)

From Morning to Evening:

a Book for Invalids.

From the French of M. L'Abbé Henri Perreyve. Translated and adapted by an Associate of the Sisterhood of S. John Baptist, Clewer.
Crown 8vo. 5*s.*

Popular Objections to the Book of

Common Prayer considered, in Four Sermons on the Sunday Lessons in Lent, the Commination Service, and the Athanasian Creed, with a Preface on the existing Lectionary.

By **Edward Meyrick Goulburn**, D.D., Dean of Norwich.
Second Edition. Small 8vo. 2*s.* 6*d.*

Family Prayers: compiled from various

sources (chiefly from Bishop Hamilton's Manual), and arranged on the Liturgical Principle.

By **Edward Meyrick Goulburn**, D.D., Dean of Norwich.
New Edition. Crown 8vo, large type, 3*s.* 6*d.*
Cheap Edition. 16mo. 1*s.*

The Annual Register: a Review of

Public Events at Home and Abroad, for the Year 1869; being the Seventh Volume of an improved Series.
8vo. 18*s.*

*** *The Volumes for* 1863 *to* 1868 *may be had, price* 18*s. each.*

A Prose Translation of Virgil's Ec-

logues and Georgics.

By an Oxford Graduate.
Crown 8vo. 2*s.* 6*d.*

London, Oxford, and Cambridge

The Cambridge Paragraph Bible of the

Authorized English Version, with the Text Revised by a Collation of its Early and other Principal Editions, the Use of the Italic type made Uniform, the Marginal References Re-modelled, and a Critical Introduction prefixed.

By the Rev. **F. H. Scrivener**, M.A., Rector of St. Gerrans ; Editor of the Greek Testament, Codex Augiensis, &c.

Edited for the Syndics of the University Press.

Crown 4to. Part I.   Genesis to Solomon's Song.   15*s.*
    ,,   ,, II.   Apocrypha and New Testament.   15*s.*
    ,,   ,, III. Prophetical Books. (*In the Press.*)

On writing paper, with one column of print and margin for MS. notes.   Part I., 20*s.* ; Part II., 20*s.*

Six Short Sermons on Sin.   Lent Lectures

at S. Alban the Martyr, Holborn.

By the Rev. **Orby Shipley**, M.A.

Fourth Edition. Small 8vo. 1*s.*

Herbert Tresham: a Tale of the Great

Rebellion.

By the late Rev. **J. M. Neale**, D.D., sometime Scholar of Trinity College, Cambridge, and late Warden of Sackville College, East Grinsted.

New Edition. Small 8vo. 3*s.* 6*d.*

Quiet Moments: a Four Weeks' Course

of Thoughts and Meditations, before Evening Prayer and at Sunset.

By **Lady Charlotte Maria Pepys.**

New Edition. Small 8vo. 2*s.* 6*d.*

Morning Notes of Praise:

A Series of Meditations upon the Morning Psalms.

By **Lady Charlotte Maria Pepys.**

New Edition. Small 8vo. 2*s.* 6*d.*

A Memoir of the late Henry Hoare,

Esq., M.A. With a Narrative of the Church Movements with which he was connected from 1848 to 1865, and more particularly of the Revival of Convocation.

By **James Bradby Sweet**, M.A.

8vo. 12s.

Yesterday, To-day, and For Ever: a

Poem in Twelve Books.

By **Edward Henry Bickersteth**, M.A., Vicar of Christ Church Hampstead, and Chaplain to the Bishop of Ripon.

Fourth Edition. Small 8vo. 6s.

The Perfect Man; or, Jesus an Example

of Godly Life.

By the Rev. **Harry Jones**, M.A., Incumbent of St. Luke's, Berwick Street.

Crown 8vo. 3s. 6d.

The Commentaries of Gaius.

Translated with Notes by **J. T. Abdy**, LL.D., Regius Professor of Laws in the University of Cambridge, and Barrister-at-Law of the Norfolk Circuit : formerly Fellow of Trinity Hall ; and **Bryan Walker**, M.A., M.L. ; Fellow and Lecturer of Corpus Christi College, and Law Lecturer of St. John's College, Cambridge ; formerly Law Student of Trinity Hall and Chancellor's Legal Medallist.

Crown 8vo. 12s. 6d.

Sacred Allegories :

The Shadow of the Cross—The Distant Hills—The Old Man's Home—The King's Messengers.

By the Rev. **W. Adams**, M.A., late Fellow of Merton College, Oxford.

New Edition. With Engravings from original designs by Charles W. Cope, R.A., John C. Horsley, A.R.A., Samuel Palmer, Birket Foster, and George E. Hicks.

Small 4to. 10s. 6d.

Liber Precum Publicarum Ecclesiæ
Anglicanæ.
À **Gulielmo Bright**, A.M., et **Petro Goldsmith Medd**, A.M.,
Presbyteris, Collegii Universitatis in Acad. Oxon. Sociis, Latine
redditus.
New Edition, with all the Rubrics in red. Small 8vo. *6s.*

Bible Readings for Family Prayer.
By the Rev. **W. H. Ridley**, M.A., Rector of Hambleden.
Crown 8vo.
Old Testament—Genesis and Exodus. *2s.*
New Testament, *3s. 6d.* { St. Matthew and St. Mark. *2s.*
{ St. Luke and St. John. *2s.*

Devotional Commentary on the Gospel
according to S. Matthew.
Translated from the French of **Pasquier Quesnel.**
Crown 8vo. *7s. 6d.*

The Manor Farm: a Tale.
By **M. C. Phillpotts**, Author of "The Hillford Confirmation."
With Four Illustrations. Small 8vo. *3s. 6d.*

The Religion, Discipline, and Rites of
the Church of England.
· By **John Cosin**, Bishop of Durham. Written at the instance
of Edward Hyde, Earl of Clarendon. Now first published
in English. By the Rev. **Frederick Meyrick**, M.A., Rector
of Blickling and Erpingham ; Prebendary of Lincoln ; Examining Chaplain to the Lord Bishop of Lincoln. Small 8vo. *2s.*

The New Testament for English

Readers; containing the Authorized Version, with a revised English Text; Marginal References; and a Critical and Explanatory Commentary.

By **Henry Alford**, D.D., Dean of Canterbury.

2 Vols. or 4 Parts, 8vo.   54s. 6d.

Separately,

Vol. 1, Part I.—The three first Gospels, with a Map. *Second Edition.* 12s.

Vol. 1, Part II.—St. John and the Acts. *Second Edition.* 10s. 6d.

Vol. 2, Part I.—The Epistles of St. Paul, with a Map. *Second Edition.* 16s.

Vol. 2, Part II.—Hebrews to Revelation. *Second Edition.* 8vo. 16s.

Thoughts on Personal Religion; being

a Treatise on the Christian Life in its Two Chief Elements, Devotion and Practice.

By **Edward Meyrick Goulburn**, D.D., Dean of Norwich.

New Edition. Small 8vo. 6s. 6d.

An Edition for Presentation, Two Volumes, small 8vo. 10s. 6d.

Also a Cheap Edition. Small 8vo. 3s. 6d.

Instructions for the Use of Candidates

for Holy Orders and of the Parochial Clergy; with Acts of Parliament relating to the same, and Forms proposed to be used.

By **Christopher Hodgson**, M.A., Secretary to the Governors of Queen Anne's Bounty.

Ninth Edition, Revised and Enlarged. 8vo. 16s.

THE "ASCETIC LIBRARY:"

A Series of Translations of Spiritual Works for Devotional Reading from Catholic Sources.

Edited by the Rev. **Orby Shipley**, M.A.

Square Crown 8vo.

The Mysteries of Mount Calvary.

Translated from the Latin of **Antonio de Guevara**. 3s. 6d.

Preparation for Death.

Translated from the Italian of **Alfonso**, Bishop of S. Agatha. 5s.

Counsels on Holiness of Life.

Translated from the Spanish of "The Sinner's Guide" by **Luis de Granada**. 5s.

Examination of Conscience upon Special Subjects.

Translated and abridged from the French of **Tronson**. 5s.

KEYS TO CHRISTIAN KNOWLEDGE.

Small 8vo. 2s. 6d. each.

A Key to the Knowledge and Use of the Book of Common Prayer.

By **John Henry Blunt**, M.A.

A Key to the Knowledge and Use of the Holy Bible.

By **John Henry Blunt**, M.A.

A Key to the Knowledge of Church History. (Ancient.)

Edited by **John Henry Blunt**, M.A.

A Key to the Narrative of the Four Gospels.

By **John Pilkington Norris**, M.A., Canon of Bristol, formerly one of Her Majesty's Inspectors of Schools.

RIVINGTON'S DEVOTIONAL SERIES.
Elegantly printed with red borders. 16mo. 2s. 6d. each.

Thomas à Kempis, Of the Imitation of Christ.
Also a cheap Edition, without the red borders, 1s., or in Cover, 6d.

The Rule and Exercises of Holy Living.
By **Jeremy Taylor**, D.D., Bishop of Down, and Connor, and Dromore.

Also a cheap Edition, without the red borders, 1s.

The Rule and Exercises of Holy Dying.
By **Jeremy Taylor**, D.D., Bishop of Down, and Connor, and Dromore.

Also a cheap Edition, without the red borders, 1s.

*** The Holy Living and Holy Dying may be had bound together in One Volume. 5s., or without the red borders, 2s. 6d.

A Short and Plain Instruction for the better Understanding of the Lord's Supper ; to which is annexed, the Office of the Holy Communion, with proper Helps and Directions.
By **Thomas Wilson**, D.D., late Lord Bishop of Sodor and Man.   Complete Edition.

Also a cheap Edition, without the red borders, 1s., or in Cover, 6d.

Introduction to the Devout Life.
From the French of Saint Francis of Sales, Bishop and Prince of Geneva.   A New Translation.

A Practical Treatise concerning Evil Thoughts :
wherein their Nature, Origin, and Effect are distinctly considered and explained, with many Useful Rules for restraining and suppressing such Thoughts : suited to the various conditions of Life, and the several Tempers of Mankind, more especially of melancholy Persons.

By **William Chilcot**, M.A.

With Preface and Notes by **Richard Hooper**, M.A., Vicar of Upton and Aston Upthorpe, Berks.

London, Oxford, and Cambridge

Imperial 8vo. 21s.

PART I. (CONTAINING A—K).

DICTIONARY OF DOCTRINAL AND HISTORICAL THEOLOGY,

BY VARIOUS WRITERS.

EDITED BY THE

REV. JOHN HENRY BLUNT, M.A., F.S.A.,

EDITOR OF "THE ANNOTATED BOOK OF COMMON PRAYER."

————◆————

THIS is the first portion of the " Summary of Theology and Ecclesiastical History," which Messrs. Rivington propose to publish as a " Thesaurus Theologicus " for the Clergy and Reading Laity of the Church of England.

It consists of original articles on all the important Doctrines of Theology, and on other questions necessary for their further illustration, the articles being carefully written with a view to modern thought, as well as a respect for ancient authority.

Part II., completing the Dictionary, is nearly ready.

NEW PAMPHLETS

BY THE BISHOP OF ST. DAVID'S.

A Charge delivered to the Clergy of the diocese
of St. David's, at his Tenth Visitation, October and November, 1869.
With an Appendix, containing an answer to the question, What is Transub-
stantiation? *Second Edition.* 8vo. 2s. 6d.

BY THE BISHOP OF LLANDAFF.

A Charge delivered to the Clergy of the diocese of
Llandaff, at his Seventh Visitation, August, 1869. With an Appendix, containing Notes on the Doctrine of the Objective Presence. 8vo. 2s.

BY THE BISHOP OF BANGOR.

A Charge delivered to the Clergy of the diocese of
Bangor, at his Fourth Visitation, August, 1869. 8vo. 1s.

BY THE BISHOP OF ROCHESTER.

A Charge delivered to the Clergy and Churchwardens
of the diocese of Rochester, at his Primary Visitation, in October and
November, 1869. 8vo. 6d.

BY THE DEAN OF DURHAM.

The Faith and Work of a Bishop: a Sermon,
preached in Westminster Abbey, at the Consecration of the Bishops of
Exeter, Bath and Wells, and the Falkland Islands, on St. Thomas's Day,
December 21, 1869. 8vo. 1s.

BY CANON SEYMOUR.

Sisterhoods, the Fruits of Christian Love: a Sermon,
preached in St. Mark's Church, Gloucester, on the anniversary of St. Lucy's
Home and Hospital, December 13, 1869. Published by request. 8vo. 6d.

BY CANON BRIGHT.

Christ's Presence amid Theological Studies: a Ser-
mon preached in the Parish Church of Cuddesdon, on the Anniversary
Festival of Cuddesdon College. Published by desire of the Lord Bishop of
Oxford. 8vo. 6d.

London, Oxford, and Cambridge

NEW PAMPHLETS

BY CANON LIDDON.

*How to do Good : a Sermon preached in the Cathe-*dral Church of St. Paul, May 18, 1870, at the 216th Anniversary Festival of the Sons of the Clergy. 8vo. 6d.

Pauperism and the Love of God : a Sermon preached at St. Paul's, Knightsbridge, on the Second Sunday after Trinity, 1870, for the Convalescent Hospital at Ascot. Published by request. 8vo. 1s.

The Model of our New Life : a Sermon preached at the Special Evening Service in St. Paul's Cathedral on Easter Day, 1870. 8vo. 3d., or 2s. 6d. per dozen.

BY ARCHDEACON BICKERSTETH.

A Charge delivered at his Eleventh Visitation of the Archdeaconry of Buckingham, in May and June, 1870. Published by request of the Clergy and Churchwardens. 8vo. 1s.

BY THE REV. W. H. FREMANTLE.

Lay Power in Parishes ; the most needed Church Reform. 8vo. 1s.

BY THE RIGHT HON. SIR ROBERT PHILLIMORE, D.C.L.

Judgment delivered by the Right Hon. Sir Robert Phillimore, D.C.L., Official Principal of the Arches Court of Canterbury, in the case of the Office of the Judge promoted by Sheppard *v.* Bennett. Edited by Walter G. F. Phillimore, B.C.L., of the Middle Temple, Barrister-at-Law ; Fellow of All Souls' College, and Vinerian Scholar, Oxford. 8vo. s. 6d.

———◆———

The Reformation of the Church of England [A.D. 1514—1547] : a Review, Reprinted by Permission from the "Times," of February 27th and March 1st, 1869. *Second Edition.* 8vo. 6d.

London, Oxford, and Cambridge

Now Complete in Eight Volumes, crown 8vo, 5s. each.

A NEW AND UNIFORM EDITION OF

A DEVOTIONAL COMMENTARY

ON THE

GOSPEL NARRATIVE.

BY THE

Rev. ISAAC WILLIAMS, B.D.

FORMERLY FELLOW OF TRINITY COLLEGE, OXFORD.

THOUGHTS on the STUDY of the HOLY GOSPELS.

CHARACTERISTIC DIFFERENCES IN THE FOUR GOSPELS.

OUR LORD'S MANIFESTATIONS OF HIMSELF.

THE RULE OF SCRIPTURAL INTERPRETATION FURNISHED BY OUR LORD.

ANALOGIES OF THE GOSPEL.

MENTION OF ANGELS IN THE GOSPELS.

PLACES OF OUR LORD'S ABODE AND MINISTRY.

OUR LORD'S MODE OF DEALING WITH HIS APOSTLES.

CONCLUSION.

A HARMONY of the FOUR EVANGELISTS.

OUR LORD'S NATIVITY.

OUR LORD'S MINISTRY—SECOND YEAR.

OUR LORD'S MINISTRY—THIRD YEAR.

THE HOLY WEEK.

OUR LORD'S PASSION.

OUR LORD'S RESURRECTION.

London, Oxford, and Cambridge

OUR LORD'S NATIVITY.

THE BIRTH AT BETHLEHEM.   THE FIRST PASSOVER.
THE BAPTISM IN JORDAN.

OUR LORD'S MINISTRY. SECOND YEAR.

THE SECOND PASSOVER.   THE TWELVE SENT FORTH.
CHRIST WITH THE TWELVE.

OUR LORD'S MINISTRY. THIRD YEAR.

TEACHING IN GALILEE.   LAST JOURNEY FROM GALILEE TO
TEACHING AT JERUSALEM.   JERUSALEM.

THE HOLY WEEK.

THE APPROACH TO JERUSALEM.   THE DISCOURSE ON THE MOUNT OF
THE TEACHING IN THE TEMPLE.   OLIVES.
THE LAST SUPPER.

OUR LORD'S PASSION.

THE HOUR OF DARKNESS.   THE DAY OF SORROWS.
THE AGONY.   THE HALL OF JUDGMENT.
THE APPREHENSION.   THE CRUCIFIXION.
THE CONDEMNATION.   THE SEPULTURE.

OUR LORD'S RESURRECTION.

THE DAY OF DAYS.   THE APOSTLES ASSEMBLED.
THE GRAVE VISITED.   THE LAKE IN GALILEE.
CHRIST APPEARING.   THE MOUNTAIN IN GALILEE.
THE GOING TO EMMAUS.   THE RETURN FROM GALILEE.
THE FORTY DAYS.

London, Oxford, and Cambridge

CATENA CLASSICORUM,

A SERIES OF CLASSICAL AUTHORS,

EDITED BY MEMBERS OF BOTH UNIVERSITIES UNDER
THE DIRECTION OF

THE REV. ARTHUR HOLMES, M.A.

FELLOW AND LECTURER OF CLARE COLLEGE, CAMBRIDGE, LECTURER AND LATE
FELLOW OF ST. JOHN'S COLLEGE,

AND

THE REV. CHARLES BIGG, M.A.

LATE SENIOR STUDENT AND TUTOR OF CHRIST CHURCH, OXFORD, SECOND
CLASSICAL MASTER OF CHELTENHAM COLLEGE.

Crown 8vo.

The following Parts have been already published:—

SOPHOCLIS TRAGOEDIAE,

Edited by R. C. JEBB, M.A. Fellow and Assistant Tutor of Trinity
College, Cambridge.
      [Part I. The Electra.   3s. 6d.   Part II. The Ajax.   3s. 6d.

JUVENALIS SATIRAE,

Edited by G. A. SIMCOX, M.A. Fellow and Classical Lecturer of
Queen's College, Oxford.   [Thirteen Satires.   3s. 6d.

THUCYDIDIS HISTORIA,

Edited by CHARLES BIGG, M.A. late Senior Student and Tutor of
Christ Church, Oxford.   Second Classical Master of Cheltenham College.
                        [Vol. I. Books I. and II. with Introductions. 6s.

CATENA CLASSICORUM (*continued*).

DEMOSTHENIS ORATIONES PUBLICAE,

Edited by G. H. HESLOP, M.A. late Fellow and Assistant Tutor of Queen's College, Oxford. Head Master of St. Bees.
[Parts I. & II. The Olynthiacs and the Philippics. 4s. 6d.

ARISTOPHANIS COMOEDIAE,

Edited by W. C. GREEN, M.A. late Fellow of King's College, Cambridge. Classical Lecturer at Queens' College.
[Part I. The Acharnians and the Knights. 4s.
[Part II. The Clouds. 3s. 6d.
[Part III. The Wasps. 3s. 6d.

An Edition of The Archarnians and the Knights, Revised and especially adapted for Use in Schools. 4s.

ISOCRATIS ORATIONES,

Edited by JOHN EDWIN SANDYS, M.A. Fellow and Tutor of St. John's College, and Classical Lecturer at Jesus College, Cambridge.
[Part I. Ad Demonicum et Panegyricus. 4s. 6d.

A PERSII FLACCI SATIRARUM LIBER,

Edited by A. PRETOR, M.A., of Trinity College, Cambridge, Classical Lecturer of Trinity Hall. 3s. 6d.

HOMERI ILIAS,

Edited by S. H. REYNOLDS, M.A. Fellow and Tutor of Brasenose College, Oxford. [Vol. I. Books I. to XII. 6s.

TERENTI COMOEDIAE,

Edited by T. L. PAPILLON, M.A. Fellow and Classical Lecturer of Merton College, Oxford. [Part I. Andria et Eunuchus. 4s. 6d.

CATENA CLASSICORUM.

The following Parts are in course of preparation:—

PLATONIS PHAEDO,

Edited by ALFRED BARRY, D.D. late Fellow of Trinity College, Cambridge; Principal of King's College, London.

DEMOSTHENIS ORATIONES PUBLICAE,

Edited by G. H. HESLOP, M.A. late Fellow and Assistant Tutor of Queen's College, Oxford; Head Master of St. Bees.
[Part III. De Falsâ Legatione.

MARTIALIS EPIGRAMMATA,

Edited by GEORGE BUTLER, M.A. Principal of Liverpool College; late Fellow of Exeter College, Oxford.

DEMOSTHENIS ORATIONES PRIVATAE,

Edited by ARTHUR HOLMES, M.A. Fellow and Lecturer of Clare College, Cambridge.   [Part I. De Coronâ.

HORATI OPERA,

Edited by J. M. MARSHALL, M.A. Fellow and late Lecturer of Brasenose College, Oxford; one of the Masters in Clifton College.

HERODOTI HISTORIA,

Edited by H. G. WOODS, M.A. Fellow and Tutor of Trinity College, Oxford.

TACITI HISTORIAE,

Edited by W. H. SIMCOX, M.A. Fellow and Lecturer of Queen's College, Oxford.

OVIDI TRISTIA,

Edited by OSCAR BROWNING, M.A. Fellow of King's College, Cambridge; and Assistant Master at Eton College.

CICERONIS ORATIONES,

Edited by CHARLES EDWARD GRAVES, M.A. Classical Lecturer and late Fellow of St. John's College, Cambridge.
[Part I. Pro P. Sextio.